Money Kingdom of God

Six Essential Attitudes for Followers of Christ

Susan V. Vogt

Money in the Kingdom of God

Six Essential Attitudes for Followers of Christ

Susan V. Vogt

theWORD
among us®
press

The Word Among Us Press
7115 Guilford Drive
Frederick, MD 21704
www.wau.org

15 14 13 12 11   1 2 3 4 5

ISBN 978-1-59325-188-8

Nihil Obstat: The Reverend Michael Morgan, Chancellor
Censor Librorum,
June 20, 2011

Imprimatur: +Most Reverend Felipe J. Estévez, STD
Bishop of St. Augustine,
June 20, 2011

Cover Design by Heather Raffa

Made and printed in the United States of America.

Library of Congress Cataloging-in-Publication Data

Vogt, Susan.
Money in the kingdom of God : six essential attitudes for followers of Christ / Susan Vogt.
    p. cm.
ISBN 978-1-59325-188-8
1. Finance, Personal—Religious aspects--Christianity. 2. Money—Religious aspects—
Christianity. 3. Finance, Personal—Biblical teaching. 4. Money—Biblical teaching. 5. Christian
life—Biblical teaching. 6. Christian stewardship—Biblical teaching. I. Title. II. Title: Six essential
attitudes for followers of Christ.
    HG179.V66 2011
    220.8'332024--dc22
                        2011016224

Contents

Welcome to
The Word Among Us
Keys to the Bible

Have you ever lost your keys? Everyone seems to have at least one "lost keys" story to tell. Maybe you had to break a window of your house or wait for the auto club to let you into your car. Whatever you had to do probably cost you—in time, energy, money, or all three. Keys are definitely important items to have on hand!

The guides in The Word Among Us Keys to the Bible series are meant to provide you with a handy set of keys that can "unlock" the treasures of the Scriptures for you. Scripture is God's living word. Within its pages we meet the Lord. So as we study and meditate on Scripture and unlock its many treasures, we discover the riches it contains—and in the process, we grow in intimacy with God.

Since 1982, *The Word Among Us* magazine has helped Catholics develop a deeper relationship with the Lord through daily meditations that bring the Scriptures to life. More than ever, Catholics today desire to read and pray with the Scriptures, and many have begun to form small faith-sharing groups to explore the Bible together.

We designed the Keys to the Bible series after conducting a survey among our magazine readers to learn what they wanted in a Catholic Bible study. We found that they were looking for easy-to-understand, faith-filled materials that approach Scripture from a clearly Catholic perspective. Moreover, they wanted a Bible study that could show them how they can apply what they learn from Scripture to their everyday lives. They also asked for sessions that they can complete in an hour or two.

Our goal was to design a simple, easy-to-use Bible study guide that is also challenging and thought provoking. We hope that this guide fulfills those admittedly ambitious goals. We are confident, however, that taking the time to go through this guide—whether by yourself, with a friend, or in a small group—will be a worthwhile endeavor that will bear fruit in your life.

How to Use the Guides in This Series

The study guides in the Keys to the Bible series are divided into six sessions that each deal with a particular aspect of the topic. Before starting the first session, take the time to read the introduction, which sets the stage for the sessions that follow.

Whether you use this guide for personal reflection and study, as part of a faith-sharing group, or as an aid in your prayer time, be sure to begin each session with prayer. Ask God to open his word to you and to speak to you personally. Read each Scripture passage slowly and carefully. Then, take as much time as you need to meditate on the passage and pursue any thoughts it brings to mind. When you are ready, move on to the accompanying commentary, which offers various insights into the text.

Two sets of questions are included in each session to help you "mine" the Scripture passage and discover its relevance to your life. Those under the heading "Understand!" focus on the text itself and help you grasp what it means. Occasionally a question allows for a variety of answers and is meant to help you explore the passage from several angles. "Grow!" questions are intended to elicit a personal response by helping you examine your life in light of the values and truths that you uncover through your study of the Scripture passage and its setting. Under the headings "Reflect!" and "Act!" we offer suggestions to help you respond concretely to the challenges posed by the passage.

Finally, pertinent quotations from the Fathers of the Church as well as insights from contemporary writers appear throughout each session. Coupled with relevant selections from the *Catechism of the Catholic Church* and information about the history, geography, and culture of first-century Palestine, these selections (called "In the Spotlight") add new layers of understanding and insight to your study.

As is true with any learning resource, this study will benefit you the most when you write your answers to the questions in the spaces provided. The simple act of writing can help you formulate your thoughts more clearly—and will also give you a record of your reflections and spiritual growth that you can return to in the future to see how much God has accomplished in your life. End your reading or study with a prayer thanking God for what you have learned—and ask the Holy Spirit to guide you in living out the call you have been given as a Christian in the world today.

Although the Scripture passages to be studied and the related verses for your reflection are printed in full in each guide (from the New Revised Standard Version: Catholic Edition), you will find it helpful to have a Bible on hand for looking up other passages and cross-references or for comparing different translations.

The format of the guides in The Word Among Us Keys to the Bible series is especially well suited for use in small groups. Some recommendations and practical tips for using this guide in a Bible discussion group are offered on pages 104–107.

We hope that *Money in the Kingdom of God* will help you to honestly assess the attitudes you bring to money and possessions in light of Christ's love and his call for your life. May it bring you into a closer walk not only with Jesus but also with all your brothers and sisters in Christ, especially those in need.

The Word Among Us Press

Introduction

Our Money and Our Faith

Several years ago the economy both in the United States and all over the world took a plunge. Plunging into the theme of money and faith is equally perilous and not for the faint-hearted. It's challenging to examine how we spend our money as well as our time. It means being honest with ourselves and taking a hard look not only at what we have but how generous we are with others. As we sincerely grow in trying to live more simply, we must especially guard against self-righteousness and judging others for purchases and decisions that differ from our own. It is a daunting task, and can only be done with prayer and the grace of God.

The goal of this Bible study is to help us look honestly at our lives today by taking direction and inspiration from the Scriptures upon which our faith is rooted. The times are different—Moses didn't have a GPS to guide him through the desert to the promised land, and Jesus didn't have the Internet to spread his words. The values, however, are the same. Yes, we are our brother's keeper. Yes, we are called to be good Samaritans, no matter what our nationality. Yes, we are to be prudent with the earth's resources. But we are also called to be generous and at times even lavish in celebrating and honoring each other. After all, Jesus provided more wine at the wedding feast of Cana (John 2:1-12) and gratefully accepted the anointing of his feet with precious oils (12:3-8).

Answering the Tough Questions

When we reflect on the topic of money and our faith, so many questions confront us. Consider how Jesus told the rich young man to "go, sell your possession, and give the money to the poor" (Matthew 19: 21). Is it wrong to accumulate wealth and be rich?

What if you work at a job that pays well? Must you move to a poor neighborhood or live in destitution to truly follow Jesus? What if you instead give a significant portion of your income to charitable causes?

Answering some of those thorny questions takes the wisdom of Solomon, but we can get started by exploring

- how to depend more fully on the grace of God;
- how to be content with what we have;
- how to stretch ourselves to be more generous with others;
- how to assess our use of money, time, and talent according to the mind of God, who loves not only us but all of creation—those people and places near to us and those we cannot see.

Wrap this all in an attitude of gratitude and humility, and we have some exciting and challenging thinking and praying to do together. So let's take a peak at the essential attitudes we need to follow Jesus more closely.

In the first session, we consider providence. It's tempting to evaluate the right use of money by noticing what possessions and money we have and the cost of what we want to buy. But we can't ask how much our faith is going to cost us. We can only count its cost indirectly as we trust God to provide rather than thinking our happiness and survival depend all on our own efforts and resources. This does not mean that we sit back and do nothing. After all, Jesus condemned the lazy slave who did nothing with his one talent (Matthew 25:26-28). But we will also reflect on numerous Scripture passages that remind us to trust that God loves us enough to provide for our true needs. Sometimes it takes a while to recognize what our true needs are and how God is providing, but that's when we need to listen more closely to God's voice speaking to our hearts through Scripture, and through our friends and neighbors.

Taking Responsibility for Our Neighbor

Second, we'll consider justice. The very fact that we have discretionary money to give is a blessing and not ours to take credit for. The more we have, the more we are responsible to share. The demands of the gospel are clear and compelling in this regard: "From everyone to whom much has been given, much will be required; and from the one to whom much has been entrusted, even more will be demanded" (Luke 12:48). It is not charity when we give to those in need; it is only our responsibility. Whatever we give is probably small compared to the widow's mite (Mark 12:44).

Third, we'll consider generosity. Should we follow the rich young man and sell everything we have and give it to the poor? God does not expect us to live in destitution. But if we struggle with generosity, it may help us to become more familiar with the poor. Certainly if we went to a Third World country, we would see abject poverty and illnesses that could be prevented or cured with enough money. Certainly there are also too many pockets of poverty in the Western world. We can't all go to a Third World country to realize our bounty, but most North Americans can make an effort to be in contact with someone who has less food, clothing, shelter, or access to education or health care than we do. Perhaps taking a walk or ride through a poor neighborhood, reading a book about the poor, or watching a TV special on poverty can put you in solidarity with those who have less. It doesn't mean we become poor, but being touched by another's poverty can keep us honest about what our true needs are—and help us to become more generous as a result.

Learning How to Be Content

In the fourth session, we'll consider the importance of being content. So often, whether we feel rich or poor depends on whom we compare ourselves with. Even middle-class Americans can feel poor when they compare themselves to those who are wealthy, yet a middle-class lifestyle is extravagant compared to the life of an African peasant. "If you have your food in the refrigerator, clothes on your back, a roof overhead, and a place to sleep, you are more comfortable than 75 percent of the people in this world" (Donella Meadows, *State of the Village Report*, 1990).

Our discussion about how much we own and how much we might give away has to be placed in the context of humility and gratitude, which are the topics of the fifth session. Once we realize that all we have is from God, we respond with immense gratitude. We must also remain humble even as we try to follow the gospel. Remember the words of St. Paul: "If I give away all my possessions, and if I hand over my body so that I may boast, but do not have love, I gain nothing" (1 Corinthians 13:3). The challenge to those who seek to follow Christ's words of not accumulating or relying on wealth (Mark 10:21; Luke 12:21) is to guard against self-righteousness and pride.

True voluntary simplicity means not being too full of ourselves. This may take the form of not only refraining from judging other's purchases or lifestyle, but also letting go of being right. Who really knows the needs and trials of another human being? Is it really more virtuous to fast from sweets or expensive gadgets or to fast from complaining or feeling superior?

Making Use of Our Gifts

Last, we will consider the need to invest in the kingdom of God. God has given every one of us gifts to build a better world and to bring Christ into it. How are we using our time, talent, or treasure? Are we investing it or hoarding it? Are we letting it lie fallow?

Now, let's journey together through this Bible study and see what attitudes our God might want us to bring to the topic of money. After all, he is the God who has counted the hairs on our head and promises to be with us in times of plenty and times of need—and especially in times of need.

Trusting in God

Matthew 6:25-34

[25]"Therefore I tell you, do not worry about your life, what you will eat or what you will drink, or about your body, what you will wear. Is not life more than food, and the body more than clothing? [26]Look at the birds of the air; they neither sow nor reap nor gather into barns, and yet your heavenly Father feeds them. Are you not of more value than they? [27]And can any of you by worrying add a single hour to your span of life? [28]And why do you worry about clothing? Consider the lilies of the field, how they grow; they neither toil nor spin, [29]yet I tell you, even Solomon in all his glory was not clothed like one of these. [30]But if God so clothes the grass of the field, which is alive today and tomorrow is thrown into the oven, will he not much more clothe you—you of little faith? [31]Therefore do not worry, saying, 'What will we eat?' or 'What will we drink?' or 'What will we wear?' [32]For it is the Gentiles who strive for all these things; and indeed your heavenly Father knows that you need all these things. [33]But strive first for the kingdom of God and his righteousness, and all these things will be given to you as well.

[34]"So do not worry about tomorrow, for tomorrow will bring worries of its own. Today's trouble is enough for today."

> Whoever has faith, even in the midst of difficulties, preserves that deep peace born of a trusting abandonment to the ever-provident and wise hands of God.
> —Blessed John Paul II, General Audience, February 5, 1997

This passage, often referred to as the "Lilies of the Field," is part of Jesus' famous Sermon on the Mount (Matthew 5–7) and culminates his teachings on discipleship. He has just finished talking about prayer, fasting, and almsgiving. Now he goes on to talk about how completely God will take care of us. This is not meant to lull us into passivity, however, but rather to emphasize the need to put our trust and faith fully in our loving God and not in the goods of this world. His words may console us or they may strike us as unrealistic idealism. Let's examine them more closely.

Jesus starts out by recognizing our human need for food and clothing but quickly puts these needs in context: Our life and happiness are bigger than just our material needs. He uses examples from the natural world to make his point. Indeed, doesn't it sometimes seem miraculous that tiny birds and dainty flowers survive rains, winds, heat, and cold? The same God who created nature and keeps it in existence is there for us too.

However, Jesus doesn't mean to imply that we humans can shirk work or be irresponsible. Certainly birds spend a lot of energy flapping their wings, finding seeds and grains to eat and fibers to furnish their nests. But it is the "worry" part that Jesus repeats and emphasizes. The way "worry" is used in this Scripture passage refers not so much to a psychological state as to losing focus. "What is recommended is that one's anxiety should not exceed the labor that is required to secure subsistence. It is not the use of the necessities of life that is discouraged, but the accumulation of goods. Accumulation of goods does not prolong the life of the owner as much as a cubit" (*The Jerome Biblical Commentary*).

Thus, the focus of our life needs to be on "the kingdom of God" (Matthew 6:33). When the importance we place on accumulating goods overpowers our first priority of seeking God's will, our decisions become distorted. What we own and how we can obtain even more become our goals instead of seeking and building God's kingdom.

Also at issue is the need to trust that God will provide what we really need. Again, Jesus reminds us that our heavenly Father knows that we need all these things. Jesus is not saying that we should starve ourselves and walk around without clothing. Neither does this Scripture passage mean that God will magically deliver food and clothing to our door if we but sit in prayer pondering his kingdom 24/7. Although indeed there are times when miracles like this do occur, it is not the normal way that God acts. More typically, God acts using the hands, feet, and the goodwill of other men and women to provide for those in need.

Another way to look at how God will provide for our needs is to consider that we might be called to honestly look at our "needs." Yes, we have a need for food, but how much food is sufficient for health? Yes, we have a need for clothing, but fashion can become a false god masquerading as a need.

Jesus is calling us to strengthen our faith that God is with us in good times and in bad.

By looking at how well God cares for the birds of the air and the lilies of the field, which are things we can see, Jesus reminds us that we are precious and that his Father will likewise care for us. We may say we believe this, but when our jobs are threatened, bills need to be paid, or we are sick, it is all too easy to move back into an "It-all-depends-on-me" mode. Jesus is calling us to strengthen our faith that God is with us in good times and in bad. Just as riches are not a sign of God's blessing or our own virtue, so, too, economic adversity is not necessarily a sign of moral lapse. The answer is always the same: "Strive first for the kingdom of God and his righteousness, and all these things will be given to you as well" (Matthew 6:33).

Understand!

1. Why do you suppose Jesus uses the examples of the birds of the air and lilies of the field to describe God's providential love? Why does he say that the people have "little faith" (Matthew 6:30)?

_____

_____

_____

_____

_____

_____

2. Luke 12:22-34 closely parallels this passage from Matthew. Luke, however, has a more challenging ending. What are the differences? Which rendition speaks more to you?

_____

_____

_____

_____

_____

3. Matthew compares the lilies to the splendor of reign of King Solomon (see 1 Kings 10–11), who was known not only for his wisdom but also his great wealth. How did Solomon use his wealth well, and how did it eventually corrupt him?

_____

_____

_____

_____

_____

4. What do you think Jesus meant when he said to "strive first for the kingdom of God and his righteousness"? (Matthew 6:33). Was he saying to keep the Ten Commandments? To live a life of virtue? Something more?

_____

_____

_____

_____

_____

_____

5. What might have been the worries and troubles of the people hearing Jesus words (see Matthew 6:34)? Do you think they were significantly different from the worries and troubles of people today?

_____

_____

_____

_____

_____

▶ In the Spotlight
Living in Community

Scripture scholar Dennis Hamm, SJ, says that the key to understanding Matthew 6:25-34 is verse 33: "But strive first for the kingdom of God and his righteousness, and all these things will be given to you as well":

The whole Sermon [on the Mount] is a description of the shared life of a group that has become a community because it has become a family under a heavenly Father by doing the Parent's will. An inevitable "side effect" of living that life . . . is that the needs of all (surely including food, drink, and clothing) will be met. Placing verse 33 in the context of the Father's feeding of birds and "clothing" of flowers is a way of saying that the kind of *community* to which Jesus calls his disciples is how the human creature was created to live and the ordinary means by which the Father cares for them.

The anxiety against which the teaching warns is not the prudent attention to meeting the normal needs for food, drink, and clothing. The target of the teaching is any distracting *preoccupation* with these things. . . . Doing our part in a community that is preoccupied with living the covenant of life with the Father—seeking the kingdom—liberates us from these other preoccupations. (*Building Our House on Rock: The Sermon on the Mount as Jesus' Vision for Our Lives*)

Grow!

1. What is the biggest worry you have right now? It could be lack of money, health issues, or concerns for your children or loved ones. Whatever it is, how often do you surrender that concern to God?

   _____

   _____

   _____

   _____

   _____

   _____

2. When have your worries become an obstacle to prayer, tested your faith, or distracted you from doing God's work on earth? What did you do about it?

_____

_____

_____

_____

_____

3. When have you let go of your anxieties and plunged ahead, trusting in God? If you can't think of such a time, consider an illness you recovered from, a decision you made to donate money or time you weren't sure you had, or a situation in which you allowed others to assist you. What was the result of that step in faith?

_____

_____

_____

_____

_____

4. In what ways does this Scripture passage challenge you to "let go and let God"? In what ways does it challenge you to be a more responsible steward of the gifts God has already given you? After reflecting on this reading, what might you do differently?

_____

_____

_____

_____

_____

5. Becoming a person of providence means gratefully accepting both the good and difficult times we face, trusting that God is with us through it all. It doesn't mean that God will necessarily intervene in our lives to make things easier. When have you experienced God bringing good out of evil, growth out of tragedy, or success out of failure?

_____

_____

_____

_____

_____

_____

▶ In the Spotlight
Dignity Is the Beginning of Hope

The foundation of Catholic social teaching is respect for life and the dignity of the human person. "The Catholic Church proclaims that human life is sacred and that the dignity of the human person is the foundation of a moral vision for society. This belief is the foundation of all the principles of our social teaching. . . . We believe that every person is precious, that people are more important than things, and that the measure of every institution is whether it threatens or enhances the life and dignity of the human person." (United States Catholic Conference of Bishops, *Themes of Catholic Social Teaching*).

Br. Giancarlo Bonutti, SM, joined the ministry of Mary Magdalene House when it was just getting off the ground. Mary Magdalene is a storefront where homeless men in Over-the-Rhine, an inner-city neighborhood of Cincinnati, can take a shower, get their laundry done, and receive mail to enable them to get a job. Br. Giancarlo says, "At Mary Magdalene House, we provide dignity to men. These men don't really worry and fret about what they wear as long as it's warm. But they can smell. Some are addicts. Some are mentally ill. Some are just down on their luck. The reason for their need for clothes and a shower is not important; I remember that they are precious in God's sight, which makes them worthy in my mind. I make an effort to call them each by name."

Br. Giancarlo says his work with the homeless "allows me to put flesh on our motto, 'Dignity is the beginning of hope.'" He adds, "Just as Mary of Bethany washed and anointed the feet of Jesus, our service refreshes our guests in body, mind, and spirit and enables them to face another day."

Giancarlo is just one of legions of volunteers and low-paid staff who work in homeless shelters, soup kitchens, and crisis centers in cities and towns near you. These people are the unrecognized saints among us. They clothe and shelter those who would like to toil for a wage but can't find work. You probably know some Giancarlos by other names. Perhaps you are one yourself.

Reflect!

1. If the weather and your environment are conducive, spend some time outside gazing on nature. Notice the birds, plants, grass, or even insects. Pay attention for a few minutes to each living thing, including any sounds you hear it making. If the weather is cold or inclement, find a window and imagine what life is stirring secretly beneath the snow, dead leaves, or dormant desert. Even if you are indoors, listen closely to the sounds you hear—the beating of your heart, the creaking of a door, or the furnace coming on and off. Ponder how God is watching all of this action—even watching you as you watch. Remember that just as "God so clothes the grass of the field, which is alive today and tomorrow is thrown into the oven, will he not much more clothe you?" (Matthew 6:30). Give thanks for such a watchful God.

2. Several verses that immediately precede the "Lilies of the Field" passage also talk about our relationship to money, but from a more challenging angle. Slowly read these words of Jesus. Let yourself be disturbed if that challenging feeling wells up in you.

> "Do not store up for yourselves treasures on earth, where moth and rust consume and where thieves break in and steal; but store up for yourselves treasures in heaven, where neither moth nor rust consumes and where thieves do not break in and steal. For where your treasure is, there your heart will be also." (Matthew 6:19-21)

> "No one can serve two masters; for a slave will either hate the one and love the other, or be devoted to the one and despise the other. You cannot serve God and wealth." (Matthew 6:24)

Then go back to our original reading, and hold the tension between Jesus telling us not to seek wealth and reminding us that everything we need will be provided—even if it's hard to trust.

Here are several additional passages to reflect on:

> The eyes of all look to you,
>   and you give them their food in due season.
> You open your hand,
>   satisfying the desire of every living thing.
> (Psalm 145:15-16)

> How precious is your steadfast love, O God!
>   All people may take refuge
>   in the shadow of your wings.
> They feast on the abundance of your house,

and you give them drink from the
river of your delights. (Psalm 36:7-8)

▶ In the Spotlight
"The Tenderness of God"

Blessed Mother Teresa liked to demonstrate how divine providence works by telling this story about her mission in Calcutta:

> We cook for nine thousand people every day. One day one sister came and said, "Mother, there's nothing to eat, nothing to give to the people." I had no answer. And then by nine o'clock that morning, a truck full of bread came to our house. The government gives a slice of bread and milk each day to the poor children. That day—no one in the city knew why—but suddenly all the schools were closed. And all the bread came to Mother Teresa. See, God closed the schools. He would not let our people go without food. And this was the first time, I think, in their lives that they had had such good bread and so much. This way you can see the tenderness of God. (*Experiencing God with Mother Teresa*)

Act!

1. Is there at least one worry or complaint that you're willing to let go of this month? Check yourself once a week, perhaps on Sundays, to see if you're still holding on to it. Turn it over to God again if necessary.

2. Let go of something you don't need. Perhaps it means fasting from a snack or a dessert. Perhaps it means looking through your closet for a piece of clothing that could clothe someone else, or a piece of baby equipment you are no longer using. Stop procrastinating, and actually make the trip to a St. Vincent de Paul Center or Goodwill so that you can be the hand of God to another.

▶ In the Spotlight
"Always Asking, and Always Receiving"

Dorothy Day saw the face of God in the midst of the urban poor. In 1934, Day, in conjunction with her mentor, Peter Maurin, was moved to set up Catholic Worker Houses of Hospitality to feed and clothe the poor. Day also published a weekly tabloid, *The Catholic Worker*, which not only complained loudly about injustice but also challenged people to live the gospel radically. Like Mother Teresa, Day relied on divine providence to provide for her guests, who some complained were drunks and "good-for-nothings." Asked how long her guests were permitted to stay, Dorothy, with a fierce look in her eyes, replied, "They live with us, they die with us, and we give them a Christian burial. We pray for them after they are dead. Once they are taken in, they become members of the family. Or rather they always were members of the family. They are our brothers and sisters in Christ" (*Dorothy Day: A Saint for Our Age?*). Here is what she wrote about the group's dependence on God's providence:

Our cash box is empty. We just collected the last pennies for a ball of twine and stamps and we shall take a twenty-five-cent subscription which just came in to buy meat for a stew for supper. But the printing bill, the one hundred and sixty-five dollars of it which remains unpaid, confronts us and tries to intimidate us.

But what is one hundred and sixty-five dollars to St. Joseph, or to St. Teresa of Avila either? We refuse to be affrighted. (Though of course the printer may be, "Oh, he of little faith!")

Don Bosco tells lots of stories about needing this sum or that sum to pay the rent and other bills with and the money arriving miraculously on time. And he too was always in need, always asking, and always receiving.

A great many of our friends urge us to put our paper on a business-like basis. But this isn't a business, it's a movement. And we don't know anything about business around here anyway. Well-meaning friends say, "But people get tired of appeals." We don't believe it. Probably most of our friends live as we do, from day to day and from hand to mouth, and as they get, they are willing to give. So we shall continue to appeal and we know that the paper will go on. (*House of Hospitality*)

Today, more than seventy years later, *The Catholic Worker* is still being published.

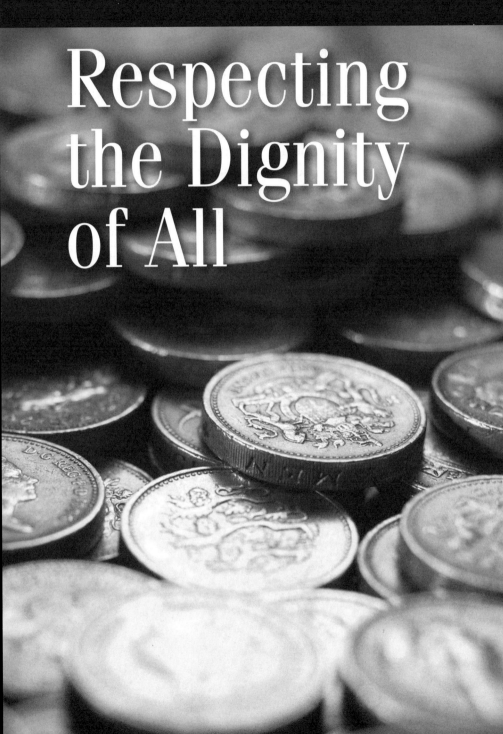

Respecting the Dignity of All

Mark 12:38-44

[38]As he taught, he said, "Beware of the scribes, who like to walk around in long robes, and to be greeted with respect in the marketplaces, [39]and to have the best seats in the synagogues and places of honor at banquets! [40]They devour widows' houses and for the sake of appearance say long prayers. They will receive the greater condemnation."

[41]He sat down opposite the treasury, and watched the crowd putting money into the treasury. Many rich people put in large sums. [42]A poor widow came and put in two small copper coins, which are worth a penny. [43]Then he called his disciples and said to them, "Truly I tell you, this poor widow has put in more than all those who are contributing to the treasury. [44]For all of them have contributed out of their abundance; but she out of her poverty has put in everything she had, all she had to live on."

> Justice will never be fully attained unless people see in the poor person, who is asking for help in order to survive, not an annoyance or a burden, but an opportunity for showing kindness and a chance for greater enrichment.
> —Blessed John Paul II, *On the Hundredth Anniversary of Rerum Novarum*

As this passage begins, we find Jesus denouncing the scribes for the pride they have taken in seeking status in the public arena. They like "to be greeted with respect in the marketplaces, and to have the best seats in the synagogues and places of honor at banquets" (Mark 12:38-39). He specifically points out their unjust treatment of widows through the taking of their property (12:40). Holding up the lowly, unobtrusive widow in the next paragraph, therefore, is quite a contrast. The scribes are condemned for taking advantage of widows while the widow is praised for her sacrifice. The injustice of the scribes is juxtaposed with the sacrificial giving of the widow.

Consider how Jesus has been sitting in the courtyard near the Temple, teaching and watching all of this. He must have been observant and astute to notice the widow's donation and then use that action as a teachable moment with his followers.

Although we don't know exactly what the equivalent of the two small copper coins would be today, we do know that those coins were the smallest currency of Jesus' day—equal to one sixty-fourth of a day's wage. Thus, comparing it to a penny in U.S. currency makes sense. That's not much—and certainly much less than the alms of the rich people who preceded the widow. The important thing, however, is not how much the coins were worth but rather that it was all the widow had.

The widow went beyond justice to self-sacrifice. In giving her two small coins—all she had to live on—she indeed gave her life for others. It may sound reckless or even irresponsible to us to give away our last penny. But it's not just about money. Perhaps the widow was able to trust in the justice of others: Just as she was generous, others would be generous with her. Intuitively, the widow must have trusted in the goodness of humanity, believing that her people would follow Jesus' commandment to "Do to others as you would have them do to you" (Luke 6:31).

One of the ways that the Jewish people traditionally honored God was by tithing—voluntarily returning the first fruits of the land to God (Numbers 18:12-13). The widow may have counted on the custom of observant Jews to care for "the Levites, . . . the resident aliens, the orphans, and the widows" (Deuteronomy 14:29). Tithing typically refers to offering 10 percent of one's income to God, but the percentage is not as important as remembering that everything we have, indeed all of creation, is a gift from God, and thus it is only right and just that we return a portion to the Lord.

Being a widow, this woman must have known suffering—the emotional suffering of losing a husband and the physical suffering of being poor. Suffering often softens our heart to the pain of others. As one who knew what it meant to go without, she was ready to give to others in need. We hear her instincts confirmed in the words of the *Catechism*:

> **As one who knew what it meant to go without, she was ready to give to others in need.**

> Respect for the human person proceeds by way of respect for the principle that "everyone should look upon his neighbor (without any exception) as 'another self,' above all bearing in mind his life and the means necessary for living it with dignity" (*Gaudium et Spes*, 27). No legislation could by itself do away with the fears, prejudices, and attitudes of pride and selfishness which obstruct the establishment of truly fraternal societies. Such behavior will cease only through the charity that finds in every man a "neighbor," a brother. (CCC, 1931)

Ultimately, giving all that she had was an act of faith and trust in God. Although she may not have had the theological background to say, "I am created in the image and likeness of God and, therefore, I have dignity," she obviously believed that God would not abandon her. Let us pray to have the faith and trust in God of this widow, whose action has been memorialized for all time.

Understand!

1. Apparently it was common practice for Jewish people to gather around the Temple and make donations to buy oil, wine, or other provisions for the Temple sacrifices or for other Temple expenses. What clues from this passage might indicate to us that some people made a show of how much they were giving?

   _____

   _____

   _____

   _____

   _____

2. In taking widows' houses (see Mark 12:40), the scribes were directly violating Moses' command to the Jews: "You shall not abuse any widow or orphan. If you do abuse them, when they cry out to me, I will surely heed their cry" (Exodus 22:22-23). What do you think may have motivated the scribes—who knew the Hebrew Scriptures—to act as they did? How do you think they reacted to Jesus' words?

   _____

   _____

   _____

   _____

   _____

3. What additional attitudes and actions of the scribes was Jesus criticizing? Why do you think those things were so offensive to him?

   _____

   _____

_____

_____

_____

_____

4. Why do you think the widow gave "everything she had" (Mark 12:44)? Do you think her almsgiving was a lifelong practice? Why or why not?

_____

_____

_____

_____

_____

5. Although this passage doesn't explicitly say it was the widow's last two coins, it does say she lived in poverty and put in everything she had. How do you imagine the widow survived after leaving the Temple? Do you think she was forced to rely on relatives and friends?

_____

_____

_____

_____

_____

▶ In the Spotlight
Solidarity

A term used often in Catholic teachings on social justice is "solidarity." The *Catechism of the Catholic Church* says the principle of solidarity can also be "articulated in terms of 'friendship' or 'social charity'" and describes it as an "eminently Christian virtue" (1939, 1948). Here is what Blessed John Paul II said about solidarity in his 1987 encyclical *Sollicitudo Rei Socialis* (On Social Concern):

> [Solidarity] is not a feeling of vague compassion or shallow distress at the misfortunes of so many people, both near and far. On the contrary, it is a firm and persevering determination to commit oneself to the common good; that is to say to the good of all and of each individual, because we are all really responsible for all. . . . (38)
>
> The exercise of solidarity within each society is valid when its members recognize one another as persons. Those who are more influential, because they have a greater share of goods and common services, should feel responsible for the weaker and be ready to share with them all they possess. Those who are weaker, for their part, in the same spirit of solidarity, should not adopt a purely passive attitude or one that is destructive of the social fabric, but, while claiming their legitimate rights, should do what they can for the good of all. The intermediate groups, in their turn, should not selfishly insist on their particular interests, but respect the interests of others. (39)

Grow!

1. Everyone is made in the image of God and has a God-given dignity, whether it be a scribe or a widow, a doctor or a beg-

gar. Therefore, everyone deserves respect. What in our tone or demeanor conveys that we believe in the dignity of the person before us? In what other ways can we show respect to people?

_____

_____

_____

_____

_____

2. Jewish law required everyone to care for the needs of the poor. In what ways does our society care for the poor? What can you do to increase the awareness in your community or parish of people in desperate or needy circumstances?

_____

_____

_____

_____

_____

3. Whether we feel poor or rich often depends on whom we are comparing ourselves to. Compared to most people in Third World countries, most U.S. citizens are rich. Compared to Bill Gates or Warren Buffet, we probably feel like paupers. Describe an encounter you've had with someone much richer or much poorer than yourself. How did it change your perspective on your own situation? How did it help you to grow?

_____

_____

_____

_____

_____

4. How often do you stretch yourself beyond what is comfortable? Consider not only donations of money but also spending time with others or giving some of your possessions to them. What opportunities are you missing for sacrificial giving?

_____

_____

_____

_____

_____

5. Who are the "widows and orphans" in your personal life? (These can be family members as well as acquaintances.) How can viewing such people as brothers and sisters in Christ help you to better care for them?

_____

_____

_____

_____

_____

▶ In the Spotlight
St. Elizabeth of Hungary

St. Elizabeth of Hungary (1207–1231) was a wealthy princess. As was common with royalty in her day, when she was only four years old, she was betrothed to the prince of a neighboring country in what is modern-day Germany. At the age of fourteen, she married King Ludwig IV, thus uniting two kingdoms. Although St. Elizabeth had the money and power to assure herself a life of ease, she was inspired by St. Francis of Assisi to spend much of her wealth bettering the lives of the poor in her kingdom. Not only did she use her money, but she personally became involved in the lives of the sick, visiting them, binding their wounds, and eventually founding two hospitals and an orphanage. Once she even personally carried a young leper to her own room in the palace.

St. Elizabeth was the opposite of the scribes who took the property of the widows; she shared her wealth. She shared a sadness with the widow in Mark's gospel as well: She was unexpectedly widowed at the age of twenty. As palace politics would have it, Ludwig's brother became king, and St. Elizabeth and her three children were forced to leave the castle. Despite her relative fall from power, she continued her devotion to the poor and to prayer. She died at the age of twenty-four. She knew wealth and how to use it justly. She knew the loss of wealth and how to live with dignity.

Reflect!

1. The Book of Proverbs warns against laziness because it can lead to poverty. "In all toil there is profit, but mere talk leads only to poverty" (14.23). "Do not love sleep, or else you will come to poverty; open your eyes, and you will have plenty of bread" (20:13). "Anyone who tills the land will have plenty of bread, but one who follows worthless pursuits will have plenty of poverty" (28:19). Yet we can risk being judgmental if we think that people are poor only because they are lazy and do not want to work hard. What is your attitude? Do you automatically assume that people are poor through their own fault? Make an effort to reach out and develop a friendship with someone who is living in poverty. Get to know the person's specific circumstances. Then ask God to help you grow in compassion for all people who are poor.

2. Reflect on the following Scripture passages to enhance your understanding of what it means to develop an attitude of justice:

> The LORD spoke to Moses, saying: . . .
> When you reap the harvest of your land, you shall not
> reap to the very edges of your field, or gather the gleanings
> of your harvest. You shall not strip your vineyard bare, or
> gather the fallen grapes of your vineyard; you shall leave
> them for the poor and the alien: I am the LORD your God.
> You shall not steal; you shall not deal falsely; and you
> shall not lie to one another. And you shall not swear falsely
> by my name, profaning the name of your God: I am the
> LORD.
> You shall not defraud your neighbor; you shall not steal;
> and you shall not keep for yourself the wages of a laborer
> until morning. You shall not revile the deaf or put a stum-
> bling block before the blind; you shall fear your God: I am
> the Lord.
> You shall not render an unjust judgment; you shall not
> be partial to the poor or defer to the great: with justice you
> shall judge your neighbor. You shall not go around as a
> slanderer among your people, and you shall not profit by
> the blood of your neighbor: I am the LORD.
> You shall not hate in your heart anyone of your kin; you
> shall reprove your neighbor, or you will incur guilt yourself.
> You shall not take vengeance or bear a grudge against any
> of your people, but you shall love your neighbor as yourself:
> I am the LORD. (Leviticus 19:1, 9-18)

> "How long will you judge unjustly
>   and show partiality to the wicked?
> Give justice to the weak and the orphan;
>   maintain the right of the lowly and the destitute.

Rescue the weak and the needy;
   deliver them from the hand of the wicked."
(Psalm 82:2-4)

"Why do we fast, but you do not see?
   Why humble ourselves, but you do not notice?"
Look, you serve your own interest on your fast day,
   and oppress all your workers.
Look, you fast only to quarrel and to fight
   and to strike with a wicked fist. . . .
Is not this the fast that I choose:
   to loose the bonds of injustice,
   to undo the thongs of the yoke,
to let the oppressed go free,
   and to break every yoke?
Is it not to share your bread with the hungry,
   and bring the homeless poor into your house;
when you see the naked, to cover them,
   and not to hide yourself from your own kin?
(Isaiah 58:3-4, 6-7)

[Jesus said,] "But woe to you Pharisees! For you tithe mint
and rue and herbs of all kinds, and neglect justice and the
love of God; it is these you ought to have practiced, without
neglecting the others." (Luke 11:42)

▶ In the Spotlight
A Voluntary Choice

Br. Bob Donovan, SM, is a medical doctor. Doctors usually
make good incomes—even doctors who focus their practice on
the homeless, as Dr. Bob does. But he has chosen to live in an

inner-city area with the people he serves. His small apartment is uncluttered—because he doesn't have many possessions to clutter it with. Why in the world would a person who could afford to live in comfort voluntarily choose to live among the poor?

For Dr. Bob, his decision has to do with faith and a belief that for those who have more, more will be demanded. His choice is made easier because he's not alone. As part of a Marianist community committed to serving the poor, he is using his particular talents to serve those around him. Dr. Bob does not look at what he's doing as heroic or saintly; it's merely the just thing to do.

Act!

1. Pray about your charitable contributions and evaluate how just they are. Maybe you are already stretching yourself to give the maximum you can afford. It's often hard to know if you're being fair to yourself and fair to the poor and to God. Some people are overly scrupulous while others rationalize that they need an excessive economic cushion. Since it's often hard to know how much is enough and how much is too much to give, tithing can be an objective standard. It's true that 10 percent of a wealthy person's income hurts less than 10 percent of a poor person's. Pray about it and adjust accordingly—and remember the widow!

2. Have you ever volunteered to spend your time for a cause to bring about social justice? Pray about what issue moves your heart—perhaps it's the pro-life movement or prison reform. Then find out how you can support it.

▶ In the Spotlight
Giving It All Away

Dacian was a nineteen-year-old college student when his family took a trip to Chicago during his summer vacation. Here is his story:

I didn't really want to take time off from my summer job for a long weekend because I needed the money, but my parents pressured me to join the family outing. It was a Saturday evening in Grant Park, and the rest of the family was enjoying the sites of downtown Chicago. I'm not much of a sightseer, so I settled down in the park with a book. It wasn't long before a street person approached me and asked for a handout. I reached into my pocket and found that I only had one twenty-dollar bill. I shrugged and gave it to him.

Apparently word spreads fast among those looking for a handout, and soon another person approached me asking for money, and then another, and another. Since I had nothing left to give, it made it easy for me to say, "Sorry, I'm broke" to the others. I realized that while the original decision to give the twenty dollars made me pause, once I'd given it all away, I felt a lot freer. I could start to understand the appeal that some people find in making a vow of poverty. When you've given all that you have, all you have left to give is yourself.

I'm out of college now and employed as a teacher's aid at St. Francis de Sales, an inner-city elementary school. The families at my school are struggling financially, and because I don't make a lot of money, I understand what it's like to just scrape by. Sometimes I wish I had the money to upgrade my computer or get my car fixed, but then, many of our families don't even own a computer or a car. I know I can't help those families financially, but I can give of myself. In this case, that often means computer expertise in the classroom and rides whenever possible.

Spending Ourselves for Others

Mark 10:17-27

¹⁷As he was setting out on a journey, a man ran up and knelt before him, and asked him, "Good Teacher, what must I do to inherit eternal life?" ¹⁸Jesus said to him, "Why do you call me good? No one is good but God alone. ¹⁹You know the commandments: 'You shall not murder; You shall not commit adultery; You shall not steal; You shall not bear false witness; You shall not defraud; Honor your father and mother.'" ²⁰He said to him, "Teacher, I have kept all these since my youth." ²¹Jesus, looking at him, loved him and said, "You lack one thing; go, sell what you own, and give the money to the poor, and you will have treasure in heaven; then come, follow me." ²²When he heard this, he was shocked and went away grieving, for he had many possessions.

> Help one another with the generosity of the Lord, and despise no one. When you have the opportunity to do good, do not let it go by.
> —St. Polycarp

²³Then Jesus looked around and said to his disciples, "How hard it will be for those who have wealth to enter the kingdom of God!" ²⁴And the disciples were perplexed at these words. But Jesus said to them again, "Children, how hard it is to enter the kingdom of God! ²⁵It is easier for a camel to go through the eye of a needle than for someone who is rich to enter the kingdom of God." ²⁶They were greatly astounded and said to one another, "Then who can be saved?" ²⁷Jesus looked at them and said, "For mortals it is impossible, but not for God; for God all things are possible."

This young man who eagerly approaches Jesus might be very much like us. He so wants to do what is right, and indeed, he has tried very hard to follow the Ten Commandments of the Old Testament. People ordinarily undertake a Bible study such as this one with a similar motivation. They very much want to understand the Bible and thus grow closer to God. It may seem odd that Jesus' first response to the man is to slow him down—to take the young man's focus off the personality of Jesus (which by this time had attracted many people mesmerized by the miracles he worked) and direct the focus back to God the Father, the source of Jesus' goodness. The first thing we need to let go of in seeking to be good is the attachment to being *seen* as good and achieving status by our association with important people. In this beginning dialogue, Jesus empties himself by not claiming that his goodness is of his own making.

Next, Jesus draws our attention to the standard ways of being good—following the commandments given to Moses. The earnest young man says he has kept these commandments, and Jesus must have known that he was telling the truth, since he looks upon him with love. It is a love that confirms the young man's goodness but challenges him to take yet another step on the journey of following Jesus—to "sell what you own, and . . . follow me" (Mark 10:21).

Jesus is telling us that it is not enough to just avoid sin. Yes, it is right and good to not kill, commit adultery, steal, and lie, but following Jesus is more than not *harming* anyone; it is about actively using our resources and our lives to *do* good for others—and this will come at a cost. We must let go of possessions and wealth that keep us from totally following Jesus. It is not that the possessions in themselves are bad or that God wants us to live penniless and in destitution. It's that we can become attached to what we own and consider ourselves entitled to our good fortune. When our money, possessions, or what we yearn to buy becomes our god and our focus, we are no longer following Jesus. The rich young man resisted letting go and throwing in his lot fully with Jesus. He wanted to hang on to his former life.

Then Jesus says these challenging words to his disciples and to us: "How hard it will be for those who have wealth to enter the kingdom of God!" (Mark 10:23). These were especially confusing words to the Jewish followers of Jesus, since wealth was commonly seen as a sign of God's favor and a reflection of one's good character. The words are challenging to us too because we live in an upwardly mobile society that equates riches with status and power.

Jesus must have known that his statement would be a "hard sell," so he repeats his point again. According to a footnote for this passage in the NRSV Study Bible, Jesus' words could also be nuanced in this way: "How hard it is *for those who trust in riches* to enter the kingdom of God!" In other words, our trust must be in God, not in the wealth we accumulate on earth. Seen in this light, we can move more readily into a stance of generosity. The more we trust God, the less we need to protect our wealth and set our hearts on buying more. It is not our worldly wealth that will bring us eternal life but following Jesus, and Jesus continually tells us to spend ourselves for others.

> It is not our worldly wealth that will bring us eternal life but following Jesus, and Jesus continually tells us to spend ourselves for others.

And then we come to Jesus' confusing reference about a camel going through the eye of a needle (Mark 10:25). Some have tried to explain the verse by saying that the "eye of a needle" referred to a narrow gate in Jerusalem. Scripture scholars now seem to agree that "for a camel to go through the eye of a needle" means exactly that. This seems impossible. The only answer Jesus gives to this perplexing situation is to turn us back to trust in God the Father, for whom all things are possible (10:26).

This Scripture passage can leave the reader not only confused but also discouraged. Does Jesus really mean that I have to sell all that I have if I am to get to heaven? But listen closely to what he says: "Go, sell what you own, and *give the money to the poor*, and you will have treasure in heaven; *then come, follow me*" (Mark 10:21, emphasis added). Maybe the point is not so much the selling as giving money to the poor and following Jesus. Wealth can distort a person's soul so that he or she become full of pride and arrogance. This doesn't have to happen, but it can. That's why Jesus warns us that it is a great danger. When we can use whatever money and possessions we have generously for the good of our neighbor, we have become "poor in spirit," for "theirs is the kingdom of heaven" (Matthew 5:3).

Understand!

1. This challenging passage about attachment to wealth follows Jesus' more appealing invitation to welcome the little children. We are told that "whoever does not receive the kingdom of God as a little child will never enter it" (Mark 10:15). Young children are known for their simplicity, since they have no wealth of their own and depend on parents and family for survival. How would a powerless child hear Jesus' message about wealth differently from a self-sufficient rich person?

   _____

   _____

   _____

   _____

   _____

   _____

2. In this passage, Jesus is asking the young man to go beyond the tenets of the Mosaic law. In the Sermon on the Mount (Matthew 5–7), Jesus also instructs his followers to go beyond the letter of the law to its spirit. Why do you think this surprised his hearers? How do you think they may have reacted to this challenging message?

_____

_____

_____

_____

_____

_____

3. There is a slight difference between Jesus' words in Mark, "You lack one thing; go, sell . . . " (10:21), and Matthew's rendition in which the young man asks, "What do I still lack?" and Jesus replies, "If you wish to be perfect, go, sell . . . " (19:20, 21). We know that no human being is perfect. How do you understand the use of the word "perfect" in this context? Compare this to Matthew 5:48, when Jesus says, "Be perfect, therefore, as your heavenly Father is perfect."

_____

_____

_____

_____

_____

_____

4. Notice that Jesus repeats his point about how difficult it will be for the wealthy to enter the kingdom of God (Mark 10:24). Even though most of Jesus disciples were not men and women of great means, it seemed to be a troubling teaching for them

also. Why do you think this was the case? How did it challenge their preconceptions?

_____

_____

_____

_____

_____

_____

5. The disciples are left with a conundrum. They ask, "Then who can be saved?" and Jesus answers, "For mortals it is impossible, but not for God; for God all things are possible" (Mark 10:26, 27). This echoes the angel Gabriel's response to Mary at the annunciation when he says, "For nothing will be impossible with God" (Luke 1:37). How did Mary's response to these words differ from the disciples'? What can we learn from her?

_____

_____

_____

_____

_____

_____

▶ In the Spotlight
Another Rich Young Man

St. Francis of Assisi (1181–1226) is an example of a rich young man who *did* leave everything to follow Jesus. His story of growing up in a wealthy family and renouncing it all—even the clothes on his back—to embrace "Lady Poverty" is well-known. However, the deeper story is how he came to this decision. Francis had several formative encounters with poor people who touched him so much that he was motivated to let go of his wealth and his position in life to live another way.

As a young adult, Francis had sought the glory of knighthood. He was on his way to fight a war when he came across a knight so poor that he took off his own fine clothes and gave them to him. Later, when he saw beggars while on pilgrimage to Rome, he decided to give them all the money he had with him, and he exchanged clothes with one of them. Once, when he met a leper on the road, he got off his horse, kissed the man, and gave him what money he had. In the beginning, rubbing shoulders with the poor and downtrodden was not part of Francis' inherited lifestyle. He could have isolated himself in a nice home and ignored those he passed on the street. Instead, he opened his eyes to those who were suffering and let them touch his heart. Those personal encounters of love moved him closer to Jesus and provided him with the motivation to let go of his security. Although Francis' decision to throw in his lot with the poor and join them in their poverty was not easy or comfortable, the spirit of joy and freedom that he felt at living this life can teach us a great deal.

Francis was "rewarded" for wholeheartedly turning his life over to Christ with the stigmata, the wounds of Jesus on the cross. Yes, it is difficult to understand such a life, and such extreme poverty may not be our own call, but all of us are called to stretch ourselves and not let our possessions interfere with following Jesus. Impossible? Yes. But pray to know how Jesus is asking you to follow him, since "for God all things are possible" (Mark 10:27).

Grow!

1. What does it mean *not* to put your trust in riches? How much less worry or concern would you have about your finances if you saw them as transitory and viewed your true wealth as your faith in God and his promise of eternal life? What specific things could you do to grow in this area?

   _____

   _____

   _____

   _____

   _____

   _____

2. Which possessions do you have that make you feel secure? Which possessions might it be really difficult for you to part with? Why? Are there possessions that you have that you can share with others? What talents and time can you share?

   _____

   _____

   _____

   _____

   _____

   _____

3. Who are some of the most generous people you know? On what basis do you evaluate their generosity? Why do you think they have so much freedom to give what they have to others?

   _____

   _____

   _____

   _____

_____

_____

4. Generosity with our possessions presupposes a generosity of heart. How is this manifested in your life? Are you generous with your judgments, giving people the benefit of the doubt? Are you generous with your forgiveness and mercy? Are you generous with the time you give your friends and family? How can growing in this disposition help you to become more like Jesus?

_____

_____

_____

_____

_____

5. Jesus' words often challenged his listeners, and many felt uncomfortable with his messages. Here are a few: "Love your enemies" (Matthew 5:44). "Take up [your] cross and follow me" (16:24). "If you are angry with a brother or sister, you will be liable to judgment" (5:22). "Do not judge, so that you may not be judged" (7:1). Which "hard saying" of Jesus do you find most challenging to you personally? Why?

_____

_____

_____

_____

_____

▶ In the Spotlight
The Church's Love for the Poor

The Church has always cared for the poor in a special way. In Catholic social teaching, this is known as the Church's "preferential option for the poor." It calls for the Church—and its members—to have a special love and concern for those in need. Here is how the *Catechism* explains it:

> In its various forms—material deprivation, unjust oppression, physical and psychological illness and death—*human misery* is the obvious sign of the inherited condition of frailty and need for salvation in which man finds himself as a consequence of original sin. This misery elicited the compassion of Christ the Savior, who willingly took it upon himself and identified himself with the least of his brethren. Hence, those who are oppressed by poverty are the object of *a preferential love* on the part of the Church which, since her origin and in spite of the failings of many of her members, has not ceased to work for their relief, defense, and liberation through numerous works of charity which remain indispensable always and everywhere. (2448)

Another long tradition in the Church is the works of mercy:

> The *works of mercy* are charitable actions by which we come to the aid of our neighbor in his spiritual and bodily necessities. Instructing, advising, consoling, comforting are spiritual works of mercy, as are forgiving and bearing wrongs patiently. The corporal works of mercy consist especially in feeding the hungry, sheltering the homeless, clothing the naked, visiting the sick and imprisoned, and

burying the dead. Among all these, giving alms to the poor is one of the chief witnesses to fraternal charity: it is also a work of justice pleasing to God. (2447)

Reflect!

1. Wealth comes in many forms—money, time, talent, and caring relationships. Some of us have an abundance of income like the rich young man. Retired people often have more time than money. Others have skills to share. The really blessed among us have loving relationships with family members or good friends. Caring relationships can make the things we lack bearable. Jesus invites us into a loving relationship with him, just as he invited the rich young man to follow him. The young man wouldn't join Jesus because he was encumbered by his worldly possessions. They tied him down. Generosity does not mean we have to take on the life of a homeless migrant, but it does mean that the more we have, the more responsibility we have for sharing that wealth lest we regard our time and talents as possessions and assume that they are signs of our superiority. Reflect on the various ways God currently blesses you and what you have to share out of your abundance.

2. Reflect on the following Scripture passages to deepen your understanding of Jesus' teaching on the nature of wealth and the need for generosity:

> Jesus replied, "A man was going down from Jerusalem to Jericho, and fell into the hands of robbers, who stripped him, beat him, and went away, leaving him half dead. Now by chance a priest was going down that road; and when he saw him, he passed by on the other side. So likewise a Levite, when he came to the place and saw him, passed by

on the other side. But a Samaritan while traveling came near him; and when he saw him, he was moved with pity. He went to him and bandaged his wounds, having poured oil and wine on them. Then he put him on his own animal, brought him to an inn, and took care of him. The next day he took out two denarii, gave them to the innkeeper, and said, 'Take care of him; and when I come back, I will repay you whatever more you spend.' Which of these three, do you think, was a neighbor to the man who fell into the hands of the robbers?" He said, "The one who showed him mercy." Jesus said to him, "Go and do likewise." (Luke 10:30-37)

The point is this: the one who sows sparingly will also reap sparingly, and the one who sows bountifully will also reap bountifully. Each of you must give as you have made up your mind, not reluctantly or under compulsion, for God loves a cheerful giver. And God is able to provide you with every blessing in abundance, so that by always having enough of everything, you may share abundantly in every good work. As it is written, "He scatters abroad, he gives to the poor; his righteousness endures forever." He who supplies seed to the sower and bread for food will supply and multiply your seed for sowing and increase the harvest of your righteousness. You will be enriched in every way for your great generosity, which will produce thanksgiving to God through us; for the rendering of this ministry not only supplies the needs of the saints but also overflows with many thanksgivings to God. (2 Corinthians 9:6-12)

The fruit of the Spirit is love, joy, peace, patience, kindness, generosity, faithfulness, gentleness, and self-control. There is no law against such things. (Galatians 5:22-23)

▶ In the Spotlight
Gracious Hospitality

Early in my career as a family life minister, I wanted to attend a national conference in San Diego, but my office could not pay for the full cost of registration, much less the price of the hotel. Neither could I. I called the local Marriage Encounter community and asked if anyone could put me up. This was over thirty years ago, and I forget the family's name, but I still remember their generosity. Only when I got to their home did I realize that this Hispanic family had much less than I did—less space, less money, fewer beds, but more mouths to feed. Yet they were so welcoming, so kind, and so willing to let me sleep in their bed. Despite their modest, even run-down home, they had big hearts. They shared what they had, no matter how meager. I received more than housing; I received inspiration from them.

Act!

1. Walk through your house or apartment. Look with gratitude on your home regardless of how humble it may be. Consider letting go of something to which you are especially attached that would ease someone else's life. Give it away even if you feel torn. That may help you identify with the rich young man and what Jesus is calling you to—both generosity and focusing on the Lord.

2. Volunteer at a homeless shelter or another place where you come in contact with those in need. Often it is time spent with those who have less than us that helps us realize our richness as well as the dignity of the poor. If possible, spend some time talking with some of the shelter residents. Treat them with the dignity they have as children of God, and allow them to teach you what it means to trust.

▶ In the Spotlight
God Is a Generous Giver

God is a god of abundance, not a god of scarcity. Jesus reveals to us God's abundance when he offers so much bread to the people that there are twelve large baskets with leftover scraps (see John 6:5-15), and when he makes his disciples catch so many fish that their boats nearly sink (see Luke 5:1-7). God doesn't give us just enough. God gives us more than enough: more bread and fish than we can eat, more love than we dared ask for.

God is a generous giver, but we can only see and enjoy God's generosity when we love God with all our hearts, mind, and strength. As long as we say, "I will love you, God, but first show me your generosity," we will remain distant from God and unable to experience what God truly wants to give us, which is life and life in abundance.

—**Henri Nouwen,** *Bread for the Journey*

Discovering Our True Needs

Luke 12:13-21

[13]Someone in the crowd said to him, "Teacher, tell my brother to divide the family inheritance with me." [14]But he said to him, "Friend, who set me to be a judge or arbitrator over you?" [15]And he said to them, "Take care! Be on your guard against all kinds of greed; for one's life does not consist in the abundance of possessions." [16]Then he told them a parable: "The land of a rich man produced abundantly. [17]And he thought to himself, 'What should I do, for I have no place to store my crops?' [18]Then he said, 'I will do this: I will pull down my barns and build larger ones, and there I will store all my grain and my goods. [19]And I will say to my soul, Soul, you have ample goods laid up for many years; relax, eat, drink, be merry.' [20]But God said to him, 'You fool! This very night your life is being demanded of you. And the things you have prepared, whose will they be?' [21]So it is with those who store up treasures for themselves but are not rich towards God."

> The heart is rich when it is content, and it is always content when its desires are fixed on God.
> —St. Miguel Febres Cordero

In this parable, which talks about the danger of hoarding riches, Jesus speaks rather harshly of the farmer who has more than he needs and who trusts in his bounty to make him happy. Sandwiched on both sides of this parable are other words from Jesus to which we also need to listen. He has just finished assuring the crowds that they are worth more than many sparrows; none of them are forgotten in God's sight (Luke 12:6-7). In the passage that follows, Jesus goes on to remind us not to worry about what we have to eat or wear (12:22-31).

It is clear from this parable that the farmer has way more than necessary to meet his own family's needs since he intends to build a bigger barn to store his surplus. The difficult part for most Christians is to discern how much we really need. Certainly we want to be responsible and feed and clothe our family, but where does one draw the line between a "need" and a "want"? For a researcher, a high-speed Internet connection may be a legitimate need since quick access to information is vital for her work. For others, it may not be essential. For a peasant in sub-Saharan Africa, even a computer is a luxury only to be imagined. It's all very relative and also very subjective.

In striving for contentment, what is the goal for a Christian? Jesus calls us to a simple lifestyle in which we don't act as if our survival depends solely on accumulating more stuff. Yet our culture continually feeds our discontent. Twenty years ago, I was content to have a standard phone that plugged into the wall. Ten years ago, I was satisfied—and even considered it a luxury—to have one simple family cell phone. Today many of us want that cell phone to take photos, send e-mails, and sync up with our other electronic devices. It's not that we should deprive ourselves of a cell phone, but when we expect that the latest upgrade or more features will finally make us really happy and content, then we are seeking a false god.

Jesus tells us not to store up treasures on earth but rather to be "rich towards God" (Luke 12:21). What does this mean for us today? Are we lacking contentment if we have more than two cars in our family, even if some of our young adults use them daily? Perhaps it means not being attached to the vehicles and lending them freely to family and neighbors. Are we content with the vehicles we have, or do we yearn for a fancier car with more options? Is it acceptable to have an expensive possession as long as we're not attached to it and share it with others? These can be perplexing questions; discerning how we are to live and the decisions we make to buy things are not simple. When faced with uncertainty, it's always wise to return to Jesus' guidance: "But strive first for the kingdom of God and his righteousness, and all these things will be given to you as well" (Matthew 6:33).

As we struggle to simplify our lifestyles to follow Jesus' call more closely, people of goodwill can differ on how they determine what is enough and what is too much. It's very tempting at this phase in the Christian journey to become judgmental of others. Jesus does not shirk from criticizing the scribes and Pharisees for their abuse of power and clinging to status. Notice, however, that in this passage, Jesus is careful not to become the judge of the questioner's brother—"Friend, who set me to be a judge or arbitrator over you?" (Luke 12:14). So, too, we need to refrain from placing our standards of a simple Christian

> Judging others will not bring us contentment but rather the same self-righteousness for which Jesus rails against the scribes and Pharisees.

lifestyle upon others, including our relatives, our neighbors, and our friends. Judging others will not bring us contentment but rather the same self-righteousness for which Jesus rails against the scribes and Pharisees. If we continue to ask God to deliver us from greed and keep our eyes on the prize—the kingdom of God—then we can trust that God will help us to recognize our true needs and that we will be able to nurture a spirit of contentment and gratitude for what we do have.

Understand!

1. How do you interpret the tone of the question put to Jesus: "Teacher, tell my brother to divide the family inheritance with me" (Luke 12:13)? Does it seem reasonable or inappropriate? Why do you think Jesus declines to get involved in the dispute? Why, instead, does he see this question as a springboard for a "teaching moment"?

   _____

   _____

   _____

   _____

   _____

   _____

2. Notice that the landowner in this parable talks to himself: "And I will say to my soul, Soul, you have ample goods laid up for many years" (Luke 12:19). What do you think this says about where this man's focus lies? In what ways has he broken his covenant with God and his people?

   _____

   _____

   _____

   _____

   _____

3. The rich fool in the parable was looking forward to a life of ease in which he could relax, eat, drink, and be merry. If he had actually lived to see those days of relaxation, do you think he would have experienced contentment? Why or why not?

_____

_____

_____

_____

_____

_____

4. Read Matthew 6:19-21. How is this teaching of Jesus from the Sermon on the Mount similar to the message of this parable? Why do you think this was an important theme for Jesus to emphasize?

_____

_____

_____

_____

_____

_____

5. What does this parable of the rich fool in Luke 12 have to say about the transitory nature of our possessions? Of our lives on earth? Do you think that it was one of the reasons Jesus told the parable?

_____

_____

_____

_____

_____

_____

The wealthy landowner in Jesus' parable seems to have lost the sense of his relationship with the land. In Jewish tradition, God owned the land; the landowner was only the steward of the land. In Leviticus 25:23, God told Moses, "The land is mine; with me you are but aliens and tenants." No land was to be sold in perpetuity, meaning that it could not be permanently bought or sold. The Israelites were even required to observe "a Sabbath of complete rest for the land" (25:4), which was not to be cultivated every seventh year. What food came up without cultivation was for everyone—the property owner, the hired laborers, and the slaves.

In the parable of the rich fool, the landowner acted as if the land and the fruit that came forth from it were his, not gifts from God, the true landowner. How easy it is for us to fall into the same trap. When we think we are entitled to land or possessions, we don't share them so easily. When we see them as gifts from a gracious and generous God, how much more likely we are to offer them to others!

Grow!

1. Being overly concerned about the future can cause us to become hoarders or tightwads. Being unconcerned about the future can lead us to become spendthrifts, spending money we don't have. Knowing your own approach to money, in which direction do

you need to move to become a better steward of the money
God has given you?

_____

_____

_____

_____

_____

_____

2. Even if you've managed to minimize your "wants" through
reflecting on the sessions so far in this Bible study, it's still
interesting to know what your heart yearns for. Think for a few
minutes before answering this question, and then try to answer it
honestly: "If only I could have _____, I'd be happy."
Are you surprised by your desire? How can you surrender your
desire for things that are not essential over to the Lord?

_____

_____

_____

_____

_____

_____

3. Living a simple and contented life is not only about reducing our
possessions; it's also about letting go of control. The prosperous
farmer thought he could control his happiness. What do you
have difficulty giving over to God? Are there any people that
you still try to control?

_____

_____

_____

_____

_____

_____

4. Do the members of your family have different opinions about the value of a simple lifestyle and what constitutes enough or too much? Have you ever been asked to arbitrate these differences? Have you been tempted to compare your lifestyle and spending decisions with those of others? (Hint: Think especially about life transitions, such as births, marriages, and burials.)

_____

_____

_____

_____

_____

_____

5. The prosperous farmer decided that if he could save up enough security for the future, he could "relax, eat, drink, and be merry" (Luke 12:19). If you had enough savings so that you didn't need to work, what would you do with your time? How would it serve the Lord and humankind?

_____

_____

_____

_____

_____

_____

▶ In the Spotlight
The Temptation to Hoard

As fearful people, we are inclined to develop a mind-set that makes us say, "There's not enough food for everyone, so I better be sure I save enough for myself in case of emergency" or "There's not enough knowledge for everyone to enjoy; so I'd better keep my knowledge to myself, so no one else will use it" or "There's not enough love to give to everybody, so I'd better keep my friends to myself to prevent others from taking them away from me." This is a scarcity mentality. It involves hoarding whatever we have, fearful that we won't have enough to survive. The tragedy, however, is that what you cling to ends up rotting in your hands.

—Henri Nouwen, *Bread for the Journey*

Reflect!

1. The constant barrage of advertising we experience can often leave us feeling discontented with our possessions. It can also lull us into believing that having such things will make us more respected or happier. How often do you read the ads in the newspaper or on the Internet or watch advertising on television? What steps can you take to avoid being deluged with such marketing techniques?

2. Reflect on the following Scripture passages, which show us how to be content with our possessions in this life while keeping in mind what God has in store for us in the future:

> [Jesus said:] "Do not be afraid, little flock, for it is your Father's good pleasure to give you the kingdom. Sell your possessions, and give alms. Make purses for yourselves that do not wear out, an unfailing treasure in heaven, where no thief comes near and no moth destroys. For where your treasure is, there your heart will be also." (Luke 12:32-34)

> I rejoice in the Lord greatly that now at last you have revived your concern for me; indeed, you were concerned for me, but had no opportunity to show it. Not that I am referring to being in need; for I have learned to be

content with whatever I have. I know what it is to have little, and I know what it is to have plenty. In any and all circumstances I have learned the secret of being well-fed and of going hungry, of having plenty and of being in need. I can do all things through him who strengthens me. (Philippians 4:10-13)

Keep your lives free from the love of money, and be content with what you have; for he has said, "I will never leave you or forsake you." So we can say with confidence,
> "The Lord is my helper;
> I will not be afraid.
> What can anyone do to me?" (Hebrews 13:5-6)

Of course, there is great gain in godliness combined with contentment; for we brought nothing into the world, so that we can take nothing out of it; but if we have food and clothing, we will be content with these. But those who want to be rich fall into temptation and are trapped by many senseless and harmful desires that plunge people into ruin and destruction. For the love of money is a root of all kinds of evil, and in their eagerness to be rich some have wandered away from the faith and pierced themselves with many pains. (1 Timothy 6:6-10)

> Do not withhold good from those to whom it is due,
>   when it is in your power to do it.
> Do not say to your neighbor, "Go, and come again;
>   tomorrow I will give it"—when you have it
>   with you. (Proverbs 3:27-28)

▶ In the Spotlight
To Be Content

What does it mean to be content? St. Paul uses the word (*autarkēs* in Greek) several times to mean that what he has is "sufficient" or "enough" (See Philippians 4:11; 1 Timothy 6:6; 2 Corinthians 9:8). That might be a good definition for us as well. Is what we have sufficient for our needs? Is it enough? If our basic needs are being met, then we should be content—as long as we are doing God's will in our lives. Being content is a virtue that we can develop and grow in. It is the habit of looking at what we have with gratitude and looking to God rather than our possessions for our happiness. With contentment comes a sense of peace. When we know we are doing what God wants, we don't have to expend a lot of energy and worry going after things that God doesn't want us to have.

Act!

1. Is there something you desire to purchase that's not really a necessity—perhaps a new electronic gadget or a new piece of clothing? Exercise some restraint by waiting a month or two before purchasing the item. Then decide if you still want or need it.

2. Take one step to simplify your life. It could be going through your closets, pruning them of unneeded clothes and clutter. It might be simplifying your calendar so that you're not racing from one meeting to another and always feeling stressed. It could be clearing your mind of worries about the future and being more present to those with whom you live and work. Letting go in any of those ways can help you become more contented with life— but it's not easy. Pray for God to be with you in your decisions.

▶ In the Spotlight
Pride and Control or Trust in God?

We may want to live as simply as possible, but we also don't want to be tightwads. What's the difference? Some saints, such as St. Francis of Assisi and Blessed Mother Teresa of Calcutta, have literally given everything away for the sake of the kingdom and have chosen "holy poverty." Others may choose to live as simply as possible because they want to be detached from their material possessions so that they can be free to serve God.

But some people who take pride in saving every penny may not be living in a way that pleases God. The difference between being "cheap" and "simple living" is an attitude of control and pride. When someone intentionally chooses to live simply or to live in "holy poverty," that person simply trusts that God will provide what is really necessary. The tightwad takes pride in how much he or saves or how little she buys, and that pleasure is the reward. There is no need for God's providence.

Of course, living in true destitution is not honorable, nor does it respect the dignity of the human person. Because of circumstances beyond their control, some people are caught in this kind of poverty, which is not holy. Such poverty represents a call to those who have more to care for the needs of the impoverished.

Recognizing God as the Source of All

Job 1:6-22

⁶One day the heavenly beings came to present themselves before the LORD, and Satan also came among them. ⁷The LORD said to Satan, "Where have you come from?" Satan answered the LORD, "From going to and fro on the earth, and from walking up and down on it." ⁸The LORD said to Satan, "Have you considered my servant Job? There is no one like him on the earth, a blameless and upright man who fears God and turns away from evil." ⁹Then Satan answered the LORD, "Does Job fear God for nothing? ¹⁰Have you not put a fence around him and his house and all that he has, on every side? You have blessed the work of his hands, and his possessions have increased in the land. ¹¹But stretch out your hand now, and touch all that he has, and he will curse you to your face." ¹²The LORD said to Satan, "Very well, all that he has is in your power; only do not stretch out your hand against him!" So Satan went out from the presence of the LORD.

> Do you want to reach the heights of God? Take hold first of the humility of God. Put on the humility of Christ. Learn to be humble; do not grow proud.
>
> —St. Augustine

¹³One day when his sons and daughters were eating and drinking wine in the eldest brother's house, ¹⁴a messenger came to Job and said, "The oxen were plowing and the donkeys were feeding beside them, ¹⁵and the Sabeans fell on them and carried them off, and killed the servants with the edge of the sword; I alone have escaped to tell you." ¹⁶While he was still speaking, another came and said, "The fire of God fell from heaven and burned up the sheep and the servants, and consumed them; I alone have escaped to tell you." ¹⁷While he was still speaking, another came and said, "The Chaldeans formed three columns, made a raid on the camels and carried them off, and killed the servants with the edge of the sword; I alone have escaped to tell you." ¹⁸While he was still speaking, another came and said, "Your sons and daughters were eating

and drinking wine in their eldest brother's house, ¹⁹and suddenly a great wind came across the desert, struck the four corners of the house, and it fell on the young people, and they are dead; I alone have escaped to tell you."

²⁰Then Job arose, tore his robe, shaved his head, and fell on the ground and worshiped. ²¹He said, "Naked I came from my mother's womb, and naked shall I return there; the LORD gave, and the LORD has taken away; blessed be the name of the LORD." ²²In all this Job did not sin or charge God with wrongdoing.

This passage and the story that follows in the Book of Job can give us great insight into the attitudes of humility and gratitude. When so many calamities befall him, Job wonders why bad things happen to good people. But Job also gives a profound response: "The LORD gave, and the LORD has taken away; blessed be the name of the LORD" (Job 1:21). Job must have already had a deep and trusting relationship with God to voice those insightful words. It's mighty difficult to stay faithful to a God who seems to be punishing you.

But the plot thickens. God allows Job not only to face the loss of property and the anguishing deaths of his sons and daughters, but also to suffer severe physical pain in his own body. Three of Job's friends hear of his ill fortune and come to console him. If you are able, read all forty-two chapters of Job yourself. If not, let me summarize, since Job doesn't come around to full humility and understanding until the final chapter.

Job's three friends are named Eliphaz, Bildad, and Zophar. They have come from a distance to console and advise Job. Even though they mean well, they are bound by their times. The culture of the sixth and fifth centuries B.C. (during the time of the Babylonian exile) understood good fortune as a reward from God for good behavior and bad fortune as a punishment for bad behavior. The friends have a debate back and forth with Job that goes something like this:

Eliphaz: "Job, perhaps you've sinned, and that is why you're being punished. It's okay. None of us are perfect. We all sin."
Job: "But I didn't sin."
Bildad: "Job, you must have sinned. Why don't you just repent?"
Job: "My life is so terrible now; I just want to die. But I don't understand why God is doing this to me."
Zophar: "Don't worry, Job; God is lenient."
Job: "No, I'm not guilty! I don't understand. God, did I sin against you?"
Eliphaz: "Job, do you doubt God? If you're being punished, you must have sinned."
Job: "But I'm innocent."
Bildad: "Well, Job, we all know that God punishes those who sin."
Job: "But . . . "
Zophar: "Yes, since you have had all this misfortune, it must be a punishment from God."
Job: "But there are some people who are obviously wicked, and not all of them are punished."
Eliphaz: "Job, your wickedness must be great to warrant this severe a punishment."
Job: "Yes, there are wicked people on earth, but *God knows I'm innocent! Why me?*"
Bildad: "How can you be so sure of your innocence, Job? You're a mortal. Only God is perfect."
Job: "God is great, but I'm not lying. God, please tell me how I have sinned!"

Then Elihu, a mysterious younger man, enters the debate and brings a whole new perspective to the discussion. Elihu explains that Job is not completely innocent; he has taken pride in his righteousness, and his responses portray the attitude that "It's all about me." Elihu goes on to describe God's goodness and majesty.

Then God enters the discussion and addresses Job directly: "Job, who created everything? Are you finding fault with me?" At this, Job understands, humbles himself, and repents. "Then Job answered the LORD: / 'I know that you can do all things, / and that no purpose of yours can be thwarted. / . . . I have uttered what I did not understand. / . . . Therefore I despise myself, / and repent in dust and ashes'" (Job 42:2, 3, 6).

Once we realize from whom all things come, humility has a door to enter our souls.

As in any good story, Job's fortunes, family, and health are restored. This may seem too simplistic an ending, but remember the anguish and self-doubt that Job had to go through. The process of Job's struggling with his friends, within himself, and with God in order to know his true self, good and bad, is the point of the story. Humility is not about denouncing yourself but rather honestly facing your true self and recognizing who is the giver of gifts and talents.

Certainly Job endured much suffering throughout this story, but as you read the passage, focus not only on the negative. Notice how Job pushes through his suffering and comes out on the side of recognizing God as the source of his life and gifts. Once we realize from whom all things come, humility has a door to enter our souls. Our possessions, good deeds, and accomplishments are not solely a result of our own effort and virtue. Yes, we may work hard and try to do the right thing, but ultimately, we, like Job, must turn with gratitude to God who created us and has given us all that we have.

Understand!

1. Although the term "Satan" is used in the beginning of this passage, scholars don't understand him as the "devil" of later Jewish and Christian theology. Rather, this Satan, which is translated in the original Hebrew as "the satan," is like a "prosecutor who spies on men's wrongdoing and reports it to his master" (*The Jerome Biblical Commentary*). This Satan seems to have lost his initial wager with God when Job fails to curse God. Read Job 2:1-9. What additional wager did Satan make with God? What was Job's response this time?

_____

_____

_____

_____

_____

2. Why do you suppose God allowed this Satan to have Job in his power? Is a person truly holy if never tested? Can we be truly grateful if we believe that our possessions are the result of our own hard work and good behavior?

_____

_____

_____

_____

_____

3. First, Satan destroyed Job's oxen, donkeys, and farm workers. Next, he took the sheep and shepherds. Then, Job's camels and their caretakers were destroyed. Finally, Job's own children were

killed. Do the order of calamities and source of death (foreign invaders versus natural disasters) have any meaning? Why or why not?

_____

_____

_____

_____

_____

_____

4. By tearing his robe and shaving his head (Job 1:20), Job was expressing his grief in the tradition of his day. These actions were quickly followed, however, by Job's famous words "The LORD gave, and the LORD has taken away; blessed be the name of the LORD" (1:21). What does this say about Job as a "blameless and upright" man (1:1)? How do you imagine Job was able to counter his loss with praise for God and by recognizing his position as being dependent upon God?

_____

_____

_____

_____

_____

_____

5. The Book of Job is one of the world's great pieces of literature. How does it ultimately answer the question about evil and why God allows bad things to happen to good people?

_____

_____

_____

_____

▶ In the Spotlight
How Does One Pray with Humility?

In addition to speaking with his friends, Job speaks *about* God and, in the later chapters, *to* God. Our conversations with God can be full of praise, complaints, requests, or sorrow. Job covers all these bases. But it is only when he takes the attitude of humility that he starts to understand and receive peace.

Several stories from the gospels can show us how to pray with humility. In the parable of the Pharisee and the tax collector (Luke 18:9-14), the Pharisee thanks God that he is not like other men and then lists all the things he has been doing for God, such as fasting and tithing. The tax collector lowers his eyes, beats his chest, and begs for mercy. "When we pray, do we speak from the height of our pride and will, or 'out of the depths' of a humble and contrite heart (Psalm 130:1)? . . . *Humility* is the foundation of prayer" (*Catechism of the Catholic Church*, 2559).

In another story, a sinful woman approaches Jesus while he is dining at the house of Simon the Pharisee. She bathes his feet with her tears and then anoints them with oil (Luke 7:36-50). When Simon wonders why Jesus would allow this woman to touch him, he tells Simon, "Her sins, which were many, have been forgiven; hence she has shown great love" (7:47). This woman knew her need for Jesus' forgiveness and she trusted that she would receive it. We can come to Jesus in humility and repentance only when we recognize our great need, and when we receive his forgiveness and love, we respond with both love and gratitude.

Grow!

1. Job humbled himself when he recognized the glory of all creation and trusted in God's ways rather than in his own defense. When have I felt humbled in my life? What emotions welled up in me? How did I feel about God at this time?

_____

_____

_____

_____

_____

2. Have you ever suffered directly for your faith in God? Most of us are not called to be martyrs, but there can be other kinds of suffering, such as when we are mocked for our beliefs by colleagues or family, or when we deny ourselves time or money to serve others. How have these experiences affected your relationship with God? Have they drawn you closer together or caused you to doubt whether it was worth having faith?

_____

_____

_____

_____

_____

3. Who is the most humble person you know? The person can be dead or alive, but it's helpful if you've known the individual personally. What have you learned about humility and acceptance from observing this person?

_____

_____

_____

_____

_____

_____

4. It is difficult to feel grateful when you are experiencing hard times. It could be financial constraints, marital problems, rebellious children, an illness, or a failed business. Can you identify a calamity or hardship in your life that in hindsight brought you blessings or drew you closer to God? Did it make you feel grateful for the trial?

_____

_____

_____

_____

_____

_____

5. We can develop a habit of gratitude by making a conscious effort at the beginning or end of each day to remember our blessings and thank God for them. How often do you consciously look for blessings in your life? Do you look for small blessings as well as big ones?

_____

_____

_____

_____

_____

_____

▶ In the Spotlight
The Benefits of Gratitude

We know that God wants us to have grateful hearts. But did you know that being grateful also makes us happier, more generous, and less materialistic?

According to studies conducted at the University of California at Davis, grateful people report higher levels of positive emotions, life satisfaction, vitality, and optimism as well as lower levels of depression and stress. In addition, grateful individuals "place less importance on material goods; they are less likely to judge their own and others' success in terms of possessions accumulated; they are less envious of others; and are more likely to share their possessions with others relative to less grateful persons."

People with a strong disposition toward gratitude "have the capacity to be empathic and to take the perspective of others." They are considered more generous and more helpful by people in their social networks. And not surprisingly, those who regularly attend religious services and pray are more likely to be grateful and "to acknowledge a belief in the interconnectedness of all life and a commitment to and responsibility to others" (Emmons Lab, University of California, Davis).

A disposition of gratitude is good for you and good for others. Cultivate this attitude by writing down five things each day for which you are grateful. Then thank God for all the gifts that have been showered on you!

Reflect!

1. Many have noticed a growing sense of entitlement in our society in which people feel that they have a right to certain things, no matter what. Do you ever harbor such a spirit? Reflect on how a sense of entitlement prevents you from being humble and grateful.

2. How often do you take credit for your good deeds? Jesus has something to say about that when he describes how to regard the good works that we do: "We are worthless slaves; we have done only what we ought to have done" (Luke 17:10). Reflect on how the attitude of humble service is the hallmark of a disciple of Christ. Now reflect on these additional Scripture passages that teach us about humility and gratitude.:

> Do nothing from selfish ambition or conceit, but in humility regard others as better than yourselves. (Philippians 2:3)

> As God's chosen ones, holy and beloved, clothe yourselves with compassion, kindness, humility, meekness, and patience. Bear with one another and, if anyone has a complaint against another, forgive each other; just as the Lord has forgiven you, so you also must forgive. Above all, clothe yourselves with love, which binds everything together in perfect harmony. (Colossians 3:12-14)

> What does the LORD require of you but to do justice, and to love kindness, and to walk humbly with your God? (Micah 6:8)

> On the way to Jerusalem Jesus was going through the region between Samaria and Galilee. As he entered a village, ten lepers approached him. Keeping their distance, they called out, saying, "Jesus, Master, have mercy on us!" When he saw them, he said to them, "Go and show yourselves to the priests." And as they went, they were made clean. Then one of them, when he saw that he was healed, turned back, praising God with a loud voice. He prostrated himself at Jesus' feet and thanked him. And he was a Samaritan. Then Jesus asked, "Were not ten made

clean? But the other nine, where are they? Was none of them found to return and give praise to God except this foreigner?" Then he said to him, "Get up and go on your way; your faith has made you well." (Luke 17:11-19)

▶ In the Spotlight
St. Vincent de Paul

St. Vincent de Paul was born to a French peasant family. Because he was a good student, he was able to complete his studies for the priesthood quickly and was ordained at the age of twenty. Shortly afterward he wrote that his principal ambition was to be "comfortably situated." God had other plans for his life, however, and changed his heart—and his ambitions.

As Fr. Vincent was on his way to claim an inheritance in Marseille, he was captured by pirates and taken to northern Africa. There he was taken as a slave and was forced to perform hard labor in the hot sun. He was sold to several different owners. The wife of his last owner was intrigued by the songs and stories of Christianity he shared and entreated her husband to convert and return Fr. Vincent to France, which he did.

Several years later Vincent became a tutor for the children of wealthy landowners, the Gondis. Monsieur de Gondi was general of the galley slaves—condemned criminals who were chained to the oars and forced to row large wooden boats. Vincent became their chaplain. Perhaps stirred by the memories of his own experience, he reached out to these men, visiting them and caring for them spiritually and physically.

With Madame de Gondi, Vincent also encouraged women in the parish and the surrounding area to care for the needy and dying. The women became known as the "Ladies of Charity." Because Vincent saw Jesus in the poor, he eventually teamed up with several other priests to preach the gospel to them and to care for their material needs. This became the religious order of priests commonly known as the Vincentians.

Although St. Vincent never realized his goal of being "comfortably situated," he became friends with the rich and powerful of his day, which provided him with opportunities to ask for their support of his various charities and missions. With the assistance of Louise de Marillac, in 1633 he also founded the Daughters of Charity. His reputation for generosity inspired the St. Vincent de Paul Societies, which to this day are models of organized charity. For those of us who are blessed with more than we need, St. Vincent de Paul stores provide a place to pass on goods to those in need. Perhaps you can donate, serve, or shop at one of these stores.

Act!

1. To be humble means to know your true self. List your strengths and weaknesses. Ask someone who knows you well to give you feedback. How well do you know yourself? Are there any strengths or virtues that you are neglecting? Any weaknesses or vices that you need to correct?

2. Before you begin the next session, find the time to express your gratitude to five different people for things you've noticed about them that you admire. Remember the criteria for a genuine compliment: It should be true and specific.

Words from Saints and Christian Heroes

Remember with thanksgiving the blessings and providence of God. Then, filled with this good thought, you will rejoice in spirit and brimming with a feeling of goodwill wholeheartedly and with all strength glorify God, giving him from the heart praises that rise on high.
—**St. Anthony of Egypt**

In ordinary life we hardly realize that we receive a great deal more than we give, and that it is only with gratitude that life becomes rich.
—**Dietrich Bonhoeffer**

What a joy it is to receive from our friends an acknowledgment of their thanksgiving for our gifts, and is it not likely that it is a joy to the Lord also?
—**Hannah Whitall Smith**

St. Paul in all his letters gives thanks for all the good things of the earth. Let us likewise give thanks for the benefits received by ourselves and others, whether big or small.
—**St. John Chrysostom**

Using the Gifts Entrusted to Us

Matthew 25:14-30

[14][Jesus said], "For it is as if a man, going on a journey, summoned his slaves and entrusted his property to them; [15]to one he gave five talents, to another two, to another one, to each according to his ability. Then he went away. [16]The one who had received the five talents went off at once and traded with them, and made five more talents. [17]In the same way, the one who had the two talents made two more talents. [18]But the one who had received the one talent went off and dug a hole in the ground and hid his master's money. [19]After a long time the master of those slaves came and settled accounts with them. [20]Then the one who had received the five talents came forward, bringing five more talents, saying, 'Master, you handed over to me five talents; see, I have made five more talents.' [21]His master said to him, 'Well done, good and trustworthy slave; you have been trustworthy in a few things, I will put you in charge of many things; enter into the joy of your master.' [22]And the one with the two talents also came forward, saying, 'Master, you handed over to me two talents; see, I have made two more talents.'

> Girded with faith and the performance of good deeds, let us follow in his paths by the guidance of the gospel; then we shall deserve to see him who has called us into his kingdom.
> —*Rule of St. Benedict*

[23]His master said to him, 'Well done, good and trustworthy slave; you have been trustworthy in a few things, I will put you in charge of many things; enter into the joy of your master.' [24]Then the one who had received the one talent also came forward, saying, 'Master, I knew that you were a harsh man, reaping where you did not sow, and gathering where you did not scatter seed; [25]so I was afraid, and I went and hid your talent in the ground. Here you have what is yours.' [26]But his master replied, 'You wicked and lazy slave! You knew, did you, that I reap where I did not sow, and gather where I did not scatter? [27]Then you ought to have invested my money

with the bankers, and on my return I would have received what was my own with interest. [28]So take the talent from him, and give it to the one with the ten talents. [29]For to all those who have, more will be given, and they will have an abundance; but from those who have nothing, even what they have will be taken away. [30]As for this worthless slave, throw him into the outer darkness, where there will be weeping and gnashing of teeth.'"

To understand this passage, we must first address the term "talent." In English, the word commonly refers to a natural ability, and thus to interpret this passage in terms of our human talents makes sense. However, it certainly sounds like the master in the parable had actually given his slaves certain sums of money. In Jesus' day, a "talent" was an unusually large amount of money. The English word we know as "talent" is derived from the Greek word for large sums of money. So "talent" can be used to describe both our money and our abilities (*Collegeville Bible Commentary*).

Jesus' followers would have easily understood that the "worthless slave" (or "useless servant" according to other translations) was meant to refer to the scribes and Pharisees whose attitude was to keep the law exactly as it was. The scribes and Pharisees were opposed to any change or development in the Jewish religion. "It was for this that they are condemned. In this parable Jesus tells us that there can be no religion without adventure, and that God can find no use for the shut mind" (William Barclay, *The Gospel of Mathew*). This parable warns us not to let our faith stagnate. Two other lessons that can be drawn from this passage have to do with the reality that each of us is given a different gift and that we must either "use it or lose it."

First, note that the head of the household gives three different amounts to his slaves. The particular amount doesn't seem to matter; instead, it is crucial what each servant does with his talent. So, too, some of us seem to receive an abundance of talents—either in the form of money or ability. We also have different gifts, not only in amount, but in nature. Some are talented in writing, others in speaking, yet others in simply hearing the word and putting it into practice. Some of us have intellectual talents while others are better with our hands or in social situations. We differ in both which abilities we have and also how strong those abilities are. We will not be judged on how much we have but rather how we use it.

This leads us more directly into the overall theme of "use it or lose it." The master may seem harsh at the end of the parable when he takes the talent away from the lazy slave and gives it to the one who had ten talents and says, "But from those who have nothing, even what they have will be taken away" (Matthew 25:29). But it is because the slave ignored his talent, not that he only had a little, that he is punished. God is not judging us according to our results but according to our effort. If we don't make use of our talent, big or small, we will lose it. This might be compared to a person who has an able body and mind but sits around doing nothing but eating junk food and recreating all day, every day. Soon both one's body and mind get out of shape from lack of use.

> God is not judging us according to our results but according to our effort.

Thus, we are responsible as Christians for the gifts we have been given. If we have been given the gift of much money—even if it is the result of our own hard work—we are responsible for using it for the common good of humankind and for the building of God's kingdom. The more talents we are given, the more we are expected to give. If we are given the gift of intellect, we are expected to use it. To waste it by not studying or applying our intelligence to our work is to offend God. The same is true for our musical, artistic, or physical gifts. We all have some kind of gift, and it is incumbent upon each of us to make the best use we can of our abilities. It is important to remember, however, that the use of our gifts is not solely for our personal enrichment but rather for the good of the kingdom of God on earth.

The man who was going on a journey to return later (Matthew 25:14) is Jesus. He entrusted his property to the servants, who are us. When Jesus comes at the last judgment, the expectation is that we will have developed our talents and used them to tend to his earthly household, our world.

Understand!

1. Read Luke's description of this parable (titled "The Parable of the Ten Pounds," 19:11-27). What are some differences in the two renditions?

   _____

   _____

   _____

   _____

   _____

   _____

2. Often it's easier to understand the value of money by knowing how many hours, weeks, or months a person would have to work to gain it. A "talent" was worth more than fifteen years of a laborer's wages. Why do you suppose the master gave such a large amount to the three slaves? What does this say about the master? About God?

   _____

   _____

   _____

_____

_____

_____

3. The master was gone a long but indeterminate length of time before demanding an accounting from his slaves. How might the servants have used the talents given to them while the master was away? What might they have done to double the master's investment?

_____

_____

_____

_____

_____

4. The lazy slave was afraid of his master's wrath. This caused him to do nothing (Matthew 25:25). Since the master is an analogy for God, what might have prompted the lazy slave to have this punishing image of God? Do you think this image spoke to the people of Jesus' day? Why or why not?

_____

_____

_____

_____

_____

it does this parable have to say about the end-time? How
esus describe the accounting of our lives that must happen then?

_____

_____

_____

_____

_____

_____

▶ In the Spotlight
What Did Moses and Jeremiah Have in Common?

Both of these Old Testament prophets originally resisted
God's call. Moses said, "O my Lord, I have never been elo-
quent, neither in the past nor even now that you have spoken
to your servant; but I am slow of speech and slow of tongue"
(Exodus 4:10). Jeremiah said, "Ah, Lord GOD! Truly I do not
know how to speak, for I am only a boy" (Jeremiah 1:6). In
both cases they were willing to trust in God and overcame
their fears. As they walked in faith and exercised their vocation to speak to their people, they were able to bring hard
but necessary messages to the Egyptians and Israelites. Some
talents are inborn, and we merely have to nurture them as
we grow older. At other times, circumstances require that
we develop a new talent or a virtue. For example, a parent may not be patient by nature but learns to develop the
virtue of patience because his children require it. With any
God-given vocation, God will supply the gifts you need to
fulfill your call.

Grow!

1. Identify five significant gifts or talents from God that you possess. Which talents have you worked especially hard to maximize? Do you have any natural abilities that, given time and practice, you could use to contribute even more to the building of God's kingdom?

_____

_____

_____

_____

_____

_____

2. How do you decide how much of your income to invest and save for yourself and your retirement and how much to contribute to others? Do you pray about such decisions before making them? How can you be more open to investing in others while still being prudent about your own future?

_____

_____

_____

_____

_____

_____

3. When have you invested in a person? Maybe you helped educate a child by tutoring him, offering a scholarship, or teaching religious education. Maybe you helped someone gain employment by offering training or a chance at a job. Perhaps you helped

someone through a tough time by opening up your home or by working for a group such as Habitat for Humanity. Were you able to see the fruits of your investment?

_____

_____

_____

_____

_____

_____

4. Have you ever invested in systemic change to build the kingdom of God here on earth? For example, have you ever become involved in a cause or in the political process to make our society more fair and just? If not, what's holding you back? Fear? Time? Other commitments?

_____

_____

_____

_____

_____

_____

5. When Jesus comes again, what do you want this world to look like? What do you want the Church to look like? What kind of legacy will you leave from your time here on earth?

_____

_____

_____

_____

_____

_____

Blessed Nicolas Steno, Bishop and Scientist

Nicolas Steno (1638–1686), also known as Niels Steensen, was born in Denmark and raised as a Lutheran. From childhood he had a very inquisitive mind. He was a keen observer of nature and not inclined to believe anything without investigating it. He applied his skill of observation to both the natural world and to faith. A serious scientist, he eventually became known as the father of geology and was a pioneer in the field of anatomy. His investigating mind also led him to probe deeply into religion, and he eventually converted to Catholicism and then became a priest and later a bishop.

Even as a bishop, he continued to foster his scientific inquiries and did not let his status as a bishop or eminent scientist lead to a life of privilege. He was known to have sold his bishop's ring and cross to help the needy. He dressed humbly and often fasted. His scientific discoveries advanced medicine and saved lives, and his gifts as a pastor benefited the people of northern Germany. Not everyone has the gifts of Nicolas Steno, but everyone can do what he did—take the talents they have and make the most of them!

Reflect!

1. Sometimes, especially when things aren't going well, it's easy to come up with a long list of complaints about what's wrong with our lives and the world. In the passage we have studied, we are asked to do just the opposite—to look at all that we have been given and to consider how to multiply these gifts for the sake of others. If it's hard to believe that you really have been given much, just take a look around you. If you are reading this, you have sight and the ability to read. If you have a group you are

meeting with to discuss the Scriptures, you have brothers and sisters in Christ. If you have a roof over your head and shoes on your feet, you have more than many other people in our world. Stop just a moment and notice the many natural and human-made wonders that are in your sight or in your hearing. We have been entrusted with our bodies, our family and friends, and our planet. It's a lot to hold in trust, and we are responsible for using these gifts wisely. Thank God for them, and remember: "From everyone to whom much has been given, much will be required; and from the one to whom much has been entrusted, even more will be demanded" (Luke 12:48).

2. Reflect on the following Scripture passages to deepen your understanding of the use of money and learn how one might leverage money or services in a loving way:

> [Jesus said,] "Whoever is faithful in a very little is faithful also in much; and whoever is dishonest in a very little is dishonest also in much. If then you have not been faithful with the dishonest wealth, who will entrust to you the true riches? And if you have not been faithful with what belongs to another, who will give you what is your own? No slave can serve two masters; for a slave will either hate the one and love the other, or be devoted to the one and despise the other. You cannot serve God and wealth."
>
> The Pharisees, who were lovers of money, heard all this, and they ridiculed him. (Luke 16:10-14)

> [Jesus said,] "There was a rich man who was dressed in purple and fine linen and who feasted sumptuously every day. And at his gate lay a poor man named Lazarus, covered with sores, who longed to satisfy his hunger with what fell from the rich man's table; even the dogs

would come and lick his sores. The poor man died and was carried away by the angels to be with Abraham. The rich man also died and was buried. In Hades, where he was being tormented, he looked up and saw Abraham far away with Lazarus by his side. He called out, 'Father Abraham, have mercy on me, and send Lazarus to dip the tip of his finger in water and cool my tongue; for I am in agony in these flames.' But Abraham said, 'Child, remember that during your lifetime you received your good things, and Lazarus in like manner evil things; but now he is comforted here, and you are in agony. Besides all this, between you and us a great chasm has been fixed, so that those who might want to pass from here to you cannot do so, and no one can cross from there to us.' He said, 'Then, father, I beg you to send him to my father's house—for I have five brothers—that he may warn them, so that they will not also come into this place of torment.' Abraham replied, 'They have Moses and the prophets; they should listen to them.' He said, 'No, father Abraham; but if someone goes to them from the dead, they will repent.' He said to him, 'If they do not listen to Moses and the prophets, neither will they be convinced even if someone rises from the dead.'" (Luke 16:19-31)

And [Jesus] said to them, "Pay attention to what you hear; the measure you give will be the measure you get, and still more will be given you. For to those who have, more will be given; and from those who have nothing, even what they have will be taken away." (Mark 4:24-25)

▶ In the Spotlight
Building the City of God

What does the kingdom of God look like? How are we to invest in it? In his encyclical *Caritas in Veritate* (Charity in Truth), issued June 29, 2009, Pope Benedict XVI explains how we build God's kingdom on earth by caring for our neighbor:

To love someone is to desire that person's good and to take effective steps to secure it. Besides the good of the individual, there is a good that is linked to living in society: the common good. It is the good of "all of us," made up of individuals, families and intermediate groups who together constitute society. It is a good that is sought not for its own sake, but for the people who belong to the social community and who can only really and effectively pursue their good within it. To desire the *common good* and strive towards it *is a requirement of justice and charity.* . . . The more we strive to secure a common good corresponding to the real needs of our neighbors, the more effectively we love them. Every Christian is called to practice this charity, in a manner corresponding to his vocation and according to the degree of influence he wields. . . .

When animated by charity, commitment to the common good has greater worth than a merely secular and political stand would have. Like all commitment to justice, it has a place within the testimony of divine charity that paves the way for eternity through temporal action. Man's earthly activity, when inspired and sustained by charity, contributes to the building of the universal *city of God*, which is the goal of the history of the human family. In an increasingly globalized society, the common good and the effort to obtain it cannot fail to assume the dimensions of the whole human family, that is to say, the community of peoples and nations, in such a way as to shape the *earthly city* in unity and peace, rendering it to some degree an anticipation and a prefiguration of the undivided *city of God.* (7)

Act!

1. Research worthy causes that invest in the development of people. Choose one to donate to as a way of multiplying your gifts.

2. Give your time, talent, and treasure, but don't stop there. Make a point to pray for the causes and people that you are investing in. This, too, can multiply your investments.

▶ In the Spotlight
Joining Together: The Multiplier Effect

Some people leverage their gifts and talents as individuals, but many find that they can multiply their talents more effectively by joining with others who have similar values and faith but different skills and needs. "The differences among persons belong to God's plan, who wills that we should need one another. These differences should encourage charity" (CCC, 1946). If you have ever worked together with others to accomplish something, what quickly becomes evident is the way in which the gifts of various people come together to get the job done. Some have organizational gifts while others are visionaries or have social networks that are useful. Some are natural leaders while others like to be the "worker bees" and simply carry out the assignments they are given. But almost always, working together will accomplish more than working alone.

Most dioceses and many parishes offer ways to combine your money and talents for social service and ministry projects that would be difficult for any one individual to do on his or her own. Perhaps you are part of a smaller faith-sharing group that does this on a more personal basis. Some Christians feel called to live together in intentional community, sharing a life of prayer, work, study, service, and fellowship. One such community is Koinonia in Americus, Georgia, which started in 1942 and was the impetus behind Habitat for Humanity, but there are many others.

Practical Pointers for Bible Discussion Groups

A Bible discussion group is another key that can help us unlock God's word. Participating in a discussion or study group—whether through a parish, a prayer group, or a neighborhood—offers us the opportunity to grow not only in our love for God's word but also in our love for one another. We don't have to be trained Scripture scholars to benefit from discussing and studying the Bible together. Bible study groups provide environments in which we can worship and pray together and strengthen our relationships with other Christians. The following guidelines can help a group get started and run smoothly.

Getting Started

- Decide on a regular time and place to meet. Meeting on a regular basis allows the group to maintain continuity without losing momentum from the previous discussion.

- Set a time limit for each session. An hour and a half is a reasonable length of time in which to have a rewarding discussion on the material contained in each of the sessions in this guide. However, the group may find that a longer time is even more advantageous. If it is necessary to limit the meeting to an hour, select sections of the material that are of greatest interest to the group.

- Designate a moderator or facilitator to lead the discussions and keep the meetings on schedule. This person's role is to help preserve good group dynamics by keeping the discussion on track. He or she should help ensure that no one monopolizes the session and that each person—including the shyest or quietest individual—

is offered an opportunity to speak. The group may want to ask members to take turns moderating the sessions.

• Provide enough copies of the study guide for all members of the group, and ask everyone to bring a Bible to the meetings. Each session's Scripture text and related passages for reflection are printed in full in the guides, but you will find that a Bible is helpful for looking up other passages and cross-references. The translation provided in this guide is the New Revised Standard Version (Catholic Edition). You may also want to refer to other translations—for example, the New American Bible or the New Jerusalem Bible—to gain additional insights into the text.

• Try to stay faithful to your commitment, and attend as many sessions as possible. Not only does regular participation provide coherence and consistency to the group discussions, but it also demonstrates that members value one another and are committed to sharing their lives with one another.

Session Dynamics

• Read the material for each session in advance, and take time to consider the questions and your answers to them. The single most important key to any successful Bible study is having everyone prepared to participate.

• As a courtesy to all members of your group, try to begin and end each session on schedule. Being prompt respects the other commitments of the members and allows enough time for discussion. If the group still has more to discuss at the end of the allotted time, consider continuing the discussion at the next meeting.

• Open the sessions with prayer. A different person could have the responsibility of leading the opening prayer at each session. The prayer could be a spontaneous one, a traditional prayer such as the Our Father, or one that relates to the topic of that particular meeting. The members of the group might also want to begin some of the meetings with a song or hymn. Whatever you choose, ask the Holy Spirit to guide your discussion and study of the Scripture text presented in that session.

- Contribute actively to the discussion. Let the members of the group get to know you, but try to stick to the topic so that you won't divert the discussion from its purpose. And resist the temptation to monopolize the conversation so that everyone will have an opportunity to learn from one another.

- Listen attentively to everyone in the group. Show respect for the other members and their contributions. Encourage, support, and affirm them as they share. Remember that many questions have more than one answer and that the experience of everyone in the group can be enriched by considering a variety of viewpoints.

- If you disagree with someone's observation or answer to a question, do so gently and respectfully, in a way that shows that you value the person who made the comment, and then explain your own point of view. For example, rather than say "You're wrong!" or "That's ridiculous!" try something like "I think I see what you're getting at, but I think that Jesus was saying something different in this passage." Be careful to avoid sounding aggressive or argumentative. Then watch to see how the subsequent discussion unfolds. Who knows? You may come away with a new and deeper perspective.

- Don't be afraid of pauses and reflective moments of silence during the session. People may need some time to think about a question before putting their thoughts into words.

- Maintain and respect confidentiality within the group. Safeguard the privacy and dignity of each member by not repeating what has been shared during the discussion session unless you have been given permission to do so. That way everyone will get the greatest benefit out of the group by feeling comfortable enough to share on a deep, personal level.

- End the session with prayer. Thank God for what you have learned through the discussion, and ask him to help you integrate it into your life.

The Lord blesses all our efforts to come closer to him. As you spend time preparing for and meeting with your small group, be confident in the knowledge that Christ will fill you with wisdom, insight, and grace, and grant you the ability to see him at work in your daily life.

Sources and Acknowledgments

Introduction

Donella Meadows, *State of the Village Report*, www.odt.org/Pictures/ popvillage.pdf.

Session 1: Providence

Raymond E. Brown, Joseph A. Fitzmyer, Roland E. Murphy, *The Jerome Biblical Commentary, New Testament* (Englewood Cliffs, NJ: Prentice-Hall, 1968), 74.

Dennis Hamm, SJ, *Building Our House on Rock: The Sermon on the Mount as Jesus' Vision for Our Lives* (Frederick, MD: The Word Among Us Press, 2011), 193.

Jean Maalouf, *Experiencing Jesus with Mother Teresa* (Frederick, MD: The Word Among Us Press, 2006), 103–104.

Dorothy Day: A Saint for Our Age? Jim Forest, The Catholic Worker Movement, http://www.catholicworker.org/dorothyday/ canonizationtext.cfm?number=34.

Dorothy Day, *House of Hospitality* (New York: Sheed and Ward, 1939), Dorothy Day Library on the Web, http://www.catholic -worker.org/dorothyday/daytext.cfm?TextID=3.

United States Conference of Catholic Bishops, "Themes of Catholic Social Teaching," http://www.usccb.org/sdwp/projects/socialteach -ing/excerpt.shtml.

Session 2: Justice

Pope John Paul II, Encyclical Letter *Sollicitudo Rei Socialis* (On Social Concern), issued Dec. 20, 1987, http://www.vatican.va/holy_father/john_paul_ii/encyclicals/documents/hf_jp-ii_enc_30121987_sollic-itudo-rei-socialis_en.html.

Session 3: Generosity

Wayne A. Meeks, General Editor, *The Harper Collins Study Bible: New Revised Standard Version* (New York: HarperCollins Publishers, 1989), 1937, footnote c.

Henri J. M. Nouwen, *Bread for the Journey: A Daybook of Wisdom and Faith* (New York: HarperCollins Publishers, 1997), Entry for May 5.

Session 4: Contentment

Henri J. M. Nouwen, *Bread for the Journey: A Daybook of Wisdom and Faith* (New York: HarperCollins Publishers, 1997), Entry for May 6.

Session 5: Humility and Gratitude

Raymond E. Brown, Joseph A. Fitzmyer, Roland E. Murphy, *The Jerome Biblical Commentary, Old Testament* (Englewood Cliffs, NJ: Prentice-Hall, 1968), 514.

"Gratitude and Well Being," Emmons Lab, University of California, Davis, Dr. Robert Emmons, Director, http://psychology.ucdavis .edu/Labs/emmons/PWT/index.cfm?Section=4.

Session 6: Investing in the Kingdom

Daniel J. Harrington, SJ, *Collegeville Bible Commentary New Testament, Vol. 1: The Gospel According to Matthew* (Collegeville, MN: Liturgical Press), 2007, 101.

William Barclay, *The Gospel of Matthew* (Philadelphia: The Westminster Press, 1975), 323.

Pope Benedict XVI, Encyclical Letter *Caritas in Veritate* (Charity in Truth), issued June 29, 2009, http://www.vatican.va/holy_father/ benedict_xvi/encyclicals/documents/hf_ben-xvi_enc_20090629_car -itas-in-veritate_en.html.

Also in The Word Among Us Keys to the Bible Series

Six Sessions for Individuals or Groups

The Women of the Gospels: Missionaries of God's Love
Item# BTWFE9

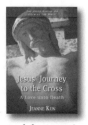

Jesus' Journey to the Cross: A Love unto Death
Item# BTWGE9

Treasures Uncovered: The Parables of Jesus
Item# BTWAE5

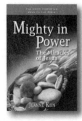

Mighty in Power: The Miracles of Jesus
Item# BTWBE6

Food from Heaven: The Eucharist in Scripture
Item# BTWCE7

Heart to Heart with God: Six Ways to Empower Your Prayer Life
Item# BTWEE8

Moved by the Spirit: God's Power at Work in His People
Item# BTWDE8

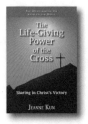

The Life-Giving Power of the Cross: Sharing in Christ's Victory
Item# BTWKE2

Each of the Keys to the Bible study sessions features

- the full Scripture text;
- a short commentary;
- questions for reflection, discussion, and personal application;
- "In the Spotlight" sections featuring wisdom from the saints and the Church, root meanings of Greek words, fascinating historical background, and stories of faith from contemporary people.

To order call 1-800-775-9673 or order online at wau.org